IMAGES
of America

GAY AND LESBIAN
PHILADELPHIA

William Penn was born in England on October 14, 1644. He had been expelled from Oxford University and imprisoned several times for radical preaching after his conversion to Quakerism. However, Penn also lived the privileged life of the landed gentry, managing his father's estates in Ireland. He first arrived in the new colonies in 1682, founding the colony he named after his deceased father and drawing up plans for his "greene Country Towne," or Philadelphia. In 1676, Penn aided the repeal of that year's capital sodomy law. The new law, known as William Penn's Great Law, abolished the death penalty for sodomy and bestiality, limiting it only for murder. Jonathan Katz in the *Gay/Lesbian Almanac* writes: "Since the earlier Quaker code of West New Jersey (1681) was silent about sodomy, this new Pennsylvania law was apparently the first in America to make sodomy a non-capital- offense." (Courtesy Free Library of Philadelphia.)

Dedicated to Steve Laverty

IMAGES
of America

GAY AND LESBIAN
PHILADELPHIA

Thom Nickels

ARCADIA

First printed in 2002.
Reprinted in 2002.

Published by Arcadia Publishing,
an imprint of Tempus Publishing, Inc.
2A Cumberland Street
Charleston, SC 29401

Printed in Great Britain.

Library of Congress Catalog Card Number: 2001099623

For all general information contact Arcadia Publishing at:
Telephone 843-853-2070
Fax 843-853-0044
E-Mail sales@arcadiapublishing.com

For customer service and orders:
Toll-Free 1-888-313-2665

Visit us on the internet at http://www.arcadiapublishing.com

Walt Whitman, America's greatest and most influential poet, lived just beyond Philadelphia in Camden, New Jersey, from 1873 until his death in 1892. Whitman revolutionized both the form and content of poetry. His use of free verse established it as an accepted form of American poetry. In the repressed atmosphere of the Victorian era, Whitman wrote seriously about the body and about loving men: "We two boys together clinging, / One the other never leaving . . ." Englishmen John Addington Symonds and Edward Carpenter, early pioneers in the area of gay self-awareness, date their coming-out to reading Whitman's Calamus poems in Leaves of Grass. Visitors to Whitman's home included English-born writer Oscar Wilde and American artist Thomas Eakins, Philadelphia's most famous painter. (Courtesy New Jersey Division of Parks and Forestry, Walt Whitman House, Camden, New Jersey, 1854 Engraving by Samuel Hollyer.)

CONTENTS

ACKNOWLEDGMENTS

This book would not have been possible without the generosity of those who went out of their way to locate personal photographs and who then took a leap of faith by letting me keep their collections for several months. The support and enthusiasm I encountered made me look at the Philadelphia gay and lesbian community with new eyes. In some cases, cynical assumptions I had made about people I heretofore did not know vanished after I listened to their stories.

Of course, no one book can be all things to all people This book is not meant to be an encyclopedic wrap-up of events and people in gay and lesbian Philadelphia since the 1800s. Space and time limitations forced me to swoop down falcon-style and take in the best or what I perceived to be important in some way. Gay and lesbian Philadelphia is such a diverse, multifaceted community that I cannot help but compare it to a complex series of highways intersecting one another in a Tower of Babel-like spiral.

My research included numerous trips to the Gay, Lesbian, Bisexual, & Transgender Archives of Philadelphia's William Way Community Center, where archivist/librarian Steven Capsuto helped me locate valuable photographs and documents donated by individuals and organizations. Capsuto, a historian himself, took special care to see that I had everything I needed and was especially helpful after I experienced some initial disappointments in my search for photographs.

Having been active in Philadelphia since 1974, my own stash of magazines, newsletters, and documents provided much information. There were old letters from Dan Sherbo and Tom Weinberg, two founders of Giovanni's Room, random issues of the *Gay Alternative* and the *Weekly Philadelphia Gayzette*, for which I was a staff writer, copies of the *Distant Drummer*, as well as the various weeklies, such as the *Philadelphia Gay News*, for which I had columns and wrote features. The pack-rat compulsion to save yielded a gold mine, though my collection was nothing compared to Robert Schoenberg's file cabinet jungle in his new West Philadelphia digs. What at first was a slim trickle of donated photographs soon mushroomed into more than I could handle, though I credit Colleen O'Connell, my editor at (the now defunct) *Au Courant* with getting the ball rolling. "Take all of our old photographs!" she told me. I could not take them all, but with my latent sifting skills I was able to pick some choice specimens.

Thanks go to Reed R. Apaghian of Philadelphia's Astral Plane restaurant, who lent me the entire Charlotte Cushman collection; Henri David, who told me some stories I cannot repeat; and Ed Hermance, who provided me with historical information and telephone numbers for people I wanted to interview. Also, thanks go to Tyrone Smith, Gail Didich, Arlene Sullivan, Pat Hill, Rita Addessa, Carlton Willers, Frank Leib, Hal Tarr, Robert Rowland, Steven Laverty, Lamont B. Steptoe, Rocco Romganoli, Dr. Marc Stein, Robert Drake of WXPN radio, John Cunningham, Tom Weinberg, Arleen Olshan, Joan C. Meyers, Jay K. Meadway of Philadelphia Volunteer Lawyers for the Arts, Karen Schwartz, Mel Heifetz, Anthony Louis, and Robert Cary Baysa.

Books were invaluable: Jonathan Katz's *Gay American History*; Marc Stein's *City of Sisterly and Brotherly Love*; John W. M. Hallocki's *Homosexuality and the Fall of Fitz-Greene Halleck*; *Sexual Heretics*; *The Spirit and the Flesh*; *The Gay Militants*; and numerous biographies and diaries.

All photography by Joan C. Meyers is copyright © Joan C. Meyers / Artists Rights Society (ARS), New York.

INTRODUCTION

During a visit to Philadelphia and Boston I noticed almost nothing of homosexuality, but visitors from those cities later assured me that there was 'an awful lot going on' within private circles in these centers of Quakerism and Puritanism . . .
—Magnus Hirschfeld, 1914

A loftier race than e'er the world hath known shall rise, with flame of freedom in their souls, and light of knowledge in their eyes.
—John Addington Symonds

Walt Whitman and writer Bayard Taylor, two notable figures in 19th-century Philadelphia, stand as examples of what it was like to be gay or lesbian in an age far different than our own.

Whitman scarcely needs an introduction; yet, there are still people who insist that the poet was not really gay. However, Oscar Wilde's impression after spending some private time with Whitman should be granted full weight. When asked by George Ives in London whether the American poet was "one of the Greek Lovers," Wilde replied, "Of course, I have the kiss of Walt Whitman still on my lips." Then, of course, there was Edward Carpenter, a former Anglican priest who claimed that he slept with Whitman and that it was Whitman's belief, as well as his own, that the way to recharge an old body was to sleep next to a young man.

Bayard Taylor, born in Kennett Square, traveled throughout Europe in lieu of a university education. He began to write poetry, but he first attracted notice when he wrote essays of his European travels for the (Philadelphia-based) *Saturday Evening Post*. Of course, being a man of his times, he became engaged to his high school sweetheart, Mary S. Agnew. The engagement, like all suspicious engagements, was a long one. What forced the marriage was Mary Agnew's coming down with tuberculosis. Taylor seemed to realize that he had little time and, sure enough, the couple had only been married for two months when she died in December 1850.

Whitman's career was a hodgepodge of newspaper editorships that came and went. He was always getting intro trouble or having personality conflicts and editorial clashes with higher-ups. Then there was his poetry—new, bold, homoerotic, and way over the Victorian "line." Taylor, on the other hand, played the journalism game according to the rules. He became "respected," even beloved. When the 1879 centennial rolled around, Whitman and Taylor both applied to write the national centennial hymn.

Whitman was hurt and even jealous when Taylor was accorded the honor. Yet, Whitman biographer Jerome Loving asks, why should he have been surprised? His writings were causing some to call him "disgusting" and "vile," and even Taylor himself called Whitman a "third-rate poet attempting to gratify his restless passion for personal notoriety." Taylor also condemned Whitman's repeated and unauthorized use of Ralph Waldo Emerson's letter as a preface in various editions of *Leaves of Grass*. He even once said that Whitman's book was not fit to "be read aloud under the evening lamp." Who knows what really motivated Taylor's attacks on the Camden poet. At the time, Taylor was a media darling, his fame worldwide; Whitman's, by contrast, lacked punch in the United States although it was beginning to grow in Europe.

Was all this merely jealous rivalry between two divas? It seems so. Taylor, actually, was no prude; he just knew how to play the polite society game. His novel *Joseph and His Friend*, which was serialized in the *Atlantic Monthly*, was the first American gay novel. Taylor even dedicated the 1869 book to those "who believe in the truth and tenderness of man's love for man, as of man's love for woman . . ."

Called "the most outspoken advocate of 'the other' [homosexual] love in mid-century America," Taylor at the time of his death not only had published some 50 books but also had just been made ambassador to Germany.

Whitman, on the other hand, had to depend on the financial kindness of strangers. Things were so bleak that, immediately following his death, urchins broke into his wine cellar and stole all the champagne. Yet Whitman is clearly better known today. His star has totally eclipsed the respected Kennett Square gentleman who, while truly great in his own right, restricted the light of truth to a contained glow under an evening lamp.

In Philadelphia, as elsewhere, life in the closet affected each gay and lesbian life differently. Some men and women lived their lives in the open, choosing to stand firm against society's unfair discrimination, while others kept their lifestyle secret from their families and friends for their entire lives.

For Charlotte Cushman, director of the Walnut Street Theater in the 1840s and an internationally acclaimed actress who specialized in playing male roles, the closet never mandated heterosexual marriage. Cushman instead had a romantic partnership with sculptor Goodhue Hosmer, as well as affairs with a number of important actresses.

The Charlotte Cushman collection contains countless photographs of young actresses who traveled to Philadelphia to appear in plays and shows. Though the identity of many of these actresses remains a mystery, many nevertheless were an integral part of Cushman's life. Cushman's intimate diary describes her profound attachment to other women, such as Eliza Cook, Matilda Hays, Geraldine Jewsbury, Sara Jane Clarke, Rosalie Kemble Sully, and Fanny Kemble. Most of these women were actresses, but many were artists and feminists.

On Philadelphia's Main Line, lesbian Bryn Mawr College president M. Carey Thomas, who turned the college into a world-class institution, once hosted a visit by Gertrude Stein. In 1869, philosopher Bertrand Russell, after a visit to the Thomas household, wrote that Thomas had "a belief in culture which she carried out with a businessman's efficiency, and a profound contempt for the male sex." Russell said that, at Bryn Mawr, Thomas "was Zeus, and everybody trembled before her." He wrote, "She lived with her friend, Miss Gwinn, who . . . used to go home to her family for three days in every fortnight, and at the exact moment of her departure each fortnight, another lady, Miss Garrett, used to arrive . . ."

During part of the 1940s, gay English scientist Alan Turing—World War II code breaker, inventor, and father of artificial intelligence—worked at the University of Pennsylvania. Turing's tragic suicide was the direct result of English homophobia, which included laws against consensual homosexual relations.

H.D. (Hilda Doolittle), the lesbian imagist poet and one-time lover of poet Ezra Pound, was briefly a Philadelphian when she met Pound at the University of Pennsylvania. Big Bill Tilden of Germantown (where there is still a Tilden Street) was the greatest tennis player in the world before his fatal weakness for ball boys got him expelled from the "Tennis Academy."

Bessie Smith, Empress of the Blues and a Philadelphia resident, suffered beatings at the hand of her husband because he disapproved of her lesbian relationships. As for the (ambiguously) bisexual painter Thomas Eakins, he shocked local philistines when he removed the posing strap from young male art models and was called "uncouth" by Philadelphia society until social mores changed. Eakins is now credited with transforming Philadelphia into an American Paris. Another notable, Violet Oakley, a painter of murals as well as the magnificent rotunda in the capitol building in Harrisburg, never hid behind the trappings of heterosexual marriage.

Although gay men and lesbians have suffered from discrimination and prejudicial violence throughout history, New York City's Stonewall Riots of 1969 helped to dismantle some of that discrimination, as well as to bring the issue of gay rights legislation into the open. Because members of the homosexual community had begun demanding their civil rights by legislation, hosts of antigay groups rallied their forces to prevent such action.

In 1974, Frank Rizzo was mayor and the city, at least in the opinion of many homosexuals, was under siege. Many called it a police state. Homophobia came packaged in the form of organizations whose goal was to defeat impending gay rights legislation. The headquarters of Neighborhood Crusades, a fundamentalist Christian social action group, was one such organization.

At the time, writer Steve Weinstock reported in the *Drummer* that the most outrageous comments in city council during hearings for Bill 1275 came from Rev. Melvin Floyd of Neighborhood Crusades. "He started off by declaring homosexuality to be morally and spiritually wrong. If the bill passed, hordes of homosexuals from New York would drift down here and take away jobs, making Philadelphia the gay capital of the nation, a line taken from a recent sensationalistic article in 'The Inquirer.' Himself a former policeman, he stated (without substantiating) that some of the worst crimes in the city were committed by homosexuals. He would not want gays to be on the police force . . . 'Suppose you call a policeman and the policeman who shows up is a homosexual. There is a man beating you up. You are half-dead on the floor. And the policeman comes in. And the man beating you up turns around and winks at him. They go together and you're half-dead on the floor. You wouldn't like it a bit.'"

The era also produced publications such as the *Gay Alternative*, the *Weekly Philadelphia Gayzette*, *New Gay Life*, as well as a variety of newsletters. Activist groups including Radical Lesbians, Radical Queens and, later, the Dyketactics hit the streets (and lives) of Philadelphians like an army of new-style Green Berets.

Frank B. Leib, author of *Friendly Competitors, Fierce Companions*, describes the founding of the Gay Liberation Front (GLF) and the life of one of its organizers, Basil O'Brien.

In the early 1970s, participation in consciousness-raising groups was a rite of passage. People with stuck prejudices were referred to as "needing their consciousness raised." Leib, O'Brien, and Kiyoshi Kuromiya, later a pioneering national leader of the AIDS movement, organized Philadelphia's first consciousness-raising group at Houston Hall at the University of Pennsylvania.

GLF was founded after the 1969 Stonewall rebellion to help liberate gay men, end racial injustice, and protest the Vietnam War. O'Brien coordinated the Philadelphia GLF meetings in an old warehouse off South Street, where participants sat on crates. Although the meetings lacked the accoutrements of a formal meeting place that similar groups enjoyed in other cities, those other groups lacked a personality as strong as O'Brien's to establish gay rights as a major political issue.

A 1974 *Philadelphia Inquirer* Sunday magazine cover story on gay and lesbian Philadelphia created a storm of controversy. The cover photograph of two dimpled white-wigged "gentlemen" with pursed red lips looked more like something out of the Marquis de Sade than serious reporting. The inside story was much worse. The essay's balanced introduction soon gave way to a tsunami of tales of sexual escapades. Activists quickly met with then *Today* magazine editor Scott DeGarmo, who told them that he "didn't see" the legitimacy of their complaints. On May 21, 1974, *Drummer* writer John Zeh reported "that the writer of the piece 'broke promises to his sources, quoted them inaccurately or when they had gone off record, and ignored much of what he was told.'"

Life was just as unpredictable on Philadelphia streets. The police under Mayor Rizzo regularly patrolled the city in vans, ordering men who looked gay into the vehicle and depositing them in jail until the next day when they were then released by a judge.

In Philadelphia, as elsewhere, the tyranny of the closet rearranged lives. The unspoken rule that, at least for a prominent personage of public or notable rank, one's sexuality, if gay or lesbian, should never be spoken of, but quietly inferred without mentioning the word.

Not naming the obvious might also be applied to the people who watch Philadelphia's annual von Steuben Day Parade every September 17. This parade honors Baron von Steuben, the Prussian general who trained George Washington's troops at Valley Forge. Not many know that von Steuben was a gay man who had fled Germany because he was about to be prosecuted for inappropriate behavior with young men—never mind the fact that he came to America with a 17-year-old French boy. Whether Washington knew of von Steuben's proclivities and cast either a blind, neutral, or approving eye in von Steuben's direction remains a mystery.

In James Lord's *A Gift for Admiration*, Henry McIlhenny, in order to keep good relations with Philadelphia society, had to put his Greek lover, Aleco, in an apartment in New York. Lord writes: "It was specified from the beginning that Aleco would not be expected to live in Philadelphia. Henry would never have accepted an arrangement which publicly proclaimed that he had provided himself with a kept boy." Philadelphia society "knew" but it didn't want the facts rubbed in its face. McIlhenny acquiesced, and trouble was avoided.

Many have said that Philadelphia suffers an inferiority complex because it is located so close to New York. After all, Philadelphia had its historic first national homosexual picket (the July 4 Annual Reminder) plucked from its cap and transported to the Big Apple one year after Stonewall cast the gay movement in militant clothes. But some things cannot be taken away: the fact that for years the largest national gay magazine of the 1960s, *Drum*, was published in Philadelphia and that the *Ladder*, the largest national lesbian magazine, was edited by a Philadelphian.

Yet, organizers of pride marches in Philadelphia never get the numbers of participants that clog the streets of New York, Chicago, Los Angeles, Boston, or even much smaller cities. Although the city has never been a marching town, emergency demonstrations over social injustices, such as the famous Burger Roasts in the 1980s, saw dedicated throngs ready to "storm the gates of the Bastille." The city's inconsistencies, while reminiscent of Whitman's "Do I contradict myself? Very well, I contradict myself . . . ," have become an accepted part of the equation, another cobblestone in Philadelphia's unique template. It's just the way we are.

—Thom Nickels

One
NEARLY INVISIBLE

The Book of Life begins with a man and a woman in a garden...It ends with Revelations.
—Oscar Wilde

American realist painter Thomas Eakins is shown *c.* 1883 in his Chestnut Street studio. While studying anatomy in Paris, Eakins observed men in athletic endeavors like rowing, boxing, swimming, and wrestling, and became interested in photography to aid him in his painting. In 1883, Eakins took a series of photographs of his nude male students diving from a jetty into a lake, which later formed the basis for his masterpiece, *The Swimming Hole.*

Eakins, who was thought by most Philadelphians to be "uncouth" and "lacking social graces," once told a class that "the male form is the most beautiful in nature." He was fired as director of the academy in 1886 when he lifted the posing strap of a male model in order to explain anatomical structure. Some students complained, and Eakins was dismissed. Though married to Susan Hannah MacDowell, Eakins met an Irish working-class boy of 17, Samuel Murray (1869–1941), and began an intense friendship that lasted 30 years. (Courtesy Pennsylvania Academy of the Fine Arts, Philadelphia. Charles Bregler's Thomas Eakins Collection. Purchased with the partial support of the Pew Memorial Trust.)

From the original painting by Chappel, in the possession of the publishers.

Johnson, Wilson & Co. Publishers, New York.

Charlotte Cushman (1816–1876) spent her childhood in Boston, where her propensity for singing to dolls led to a request to sing in a local opera. Later, Cushman switched to the stage, where she played Lady Macbeth at a New Orleans theater. Cushman believed that the theater was an excellent venue to help raise the status of women. This belief, combined with her natural instinct to dominate, led her to play mostly male roles. "I long to play a woman of strong ambition, who is at the same time very wiley and diplomatic, and who has an opportunity of a great outburst when her plans are successful—in short, a female Richelieu," Cushman wrote. Cushman was hailed in London as a great actress of her time. The Charlotte Cushman Club was founded in Philadelphia at 12th and Locust Streets in 1907. The club was also a hotel to traveling, often unaccompanied, actresses visiting Philadelphia to appear in plays. In 1909, as many as 300 actresses a week cooked in the sunny rooms and joined the Friday afternoon teas with members and managers. Cushman, herself, traveled to Philadelphia frequently for her roles in various plays. (Courtesy Charlotte Cushman Collection and Reed R. Apaghian.)

Prominent actresses of the day, such as this unnamed woman who stayed at the Cushman Club, at 12th and Locust Street, rented single rooms for rates ranging from $8 to $15 a week. An advertisement in a 1909 Plays and Players brochure called the club a place with "homelike table, perfect freedom and privacy, and with room for fourteen residents." Double rooms at the club (twin beds) ranged in price from $16 to $20 a week, including coffee and rolls, breakfast at noon, dinner at 6:00 p.m., and a midnight supper after the performance. "The club's advantages are so cheerful, pretty rooms, books and theatrical magazines, writing tables, bathrooms, telephones, a pressing and sewing room, a piano, the tea table in the attractive drawing room, a pleasant meeting place for members and friends . . ." (Courtesy Reed R. Apaghian.)

To the Cushman Club.
with best wish for
its success from
Hope Latham

Hope Latham was another of the actresses who boarded at the Cushman Club. "The girls in the show wear Stetson hats of the type under which the West made headway," a 1930 Plays and Players playbill reads. "The cowboys of the plains valued their Stetsons for the protection which they gave and for their ability to withstand hard service." In the 1920s, Philadelphia theater audiences read that, "From Paris, Monsieur Kerkoff now sends to the American ladies his incomparable Talc Djer-Kiss in this exquisite new bottle of fluted glass—a most graceful accessory for the dressing table. Here, indeed, is Talc of supreme fineness and purity. Smooth, soft as fairy gossamer. Light as thistledown . . ." "Steadily increasing numbers of women are finding the Central City Office of the Corn Exchange National Bank of advantage and convenience to them," advertisers told theatergoers in 1928. At the same time, Ann Murdock of 2104 Walnut Street was advertising scientific facial treatments that included toilet preparations, massage, and novelties.

Moreau de St. Mery was a French lawyer and politician. According to historian Jonathan Katz, when St. Mery lived in America from 1793 to 1798, he spent most of his time in Philadelphia. The lawyer's comments about lesbianism in the United States are the earliest known observations, and not surprisingly also include a negative moral judgment. "Although in general one is conscious of widespread modesty in Philadelphia, the customs are not particularly pure, and the disregard on the part of some parents for the manner in which their daughters form relationships to which they, the parents, have not given their approval is an encouragement of indiscretions which, however, are not the result of love, since American women are not affectionate.

"I am not going to say something that is almost unbelievable. These women, without real love and without passions, give themselves up at any early age to the enjoyment of themselves; and they are not at all strangers to being willing to seek unnatural pleasures with persons of their own sex." (Courtesy Cushman Collection and Reed R. Apaghian.)

Edward Carpenter's philosophy of gay male love established the groundwork for an international gay movement that influenced the work of sex researcher Havelock Ellis, novelist D.H. Lawrence, and English-born writer John Addington. Born in England in 1844, Carpenter had been ordained an Anglican priest in 1870 but left the priesthood after reading Walt Whitman's *Leaves of Grass*. He studied Hinduism, theosophy, reincarnation, and vegetarianism, and created a minor scandal by wearing sandals into the British Museum to do research. A high point in his life was his trip to America and Philadelphia to meet Walt Whitman. The meeting landed him in Whitman's bed, despite the vast difference in their ages. Carpenter, in fact, later recommended Whitman's method of sleeping next to a young man in order to recharge an old body. (Courtesy Frank B. Leib.)

Two young friends from the Philadelphia area pose *c*. 1890 before a landscape studio backdrop. In his famous 1915 book *Sexual Inversion*, Havelock Ellis wrote: "It is notable that of recent years there has been a fashion for a red tie to be adopted by inverts as their badge. This is especially marked among the 'fairies' (as a fellator is their term) in New York. 'It is red,' writes an American correspondent, himself inverted, 'that has become almost a synonym for sexual inversion, not only in the minds of inverts themselves, but in the popular mind . . . Male prostitutes who walk the streets of Philadelphia and New York almost invariably wear red neckties. It is the badge of their tribe. The rooms of many of my inverted friends have red as the prevailing color in decorations . . .'" (Courtesy Dorothy C. Nickels.)

DONCHESTER
A **Cluett** SHIRT
The Bosom cannot Bulge
$2.00

The Donchester has a bosom put on in such a way that no matter whether you sit, stand or stoop, the bosom remains flat, uncreased and in its place.

Send for the Booklet. Cluett, Peabody & Co., Makers Troy, N. Y.

PLEASE MENTION (2) PLAYS AND PLAYERS

Men's fashions were radically different at the beginning of the 20th century, as this advertisement in the October 31, 1910 Plays and Players playbill demonstrates. Time has not only altered the gender identification of the word bosom, it has given this image a camp twist, as if the illustrated men represented the tired stereotype that what a gay man really wants is to be like women. But not so far away in New Jersey and New York, Edward Hyde, Lord Cornbury, a heterosexual man, became the cross-dressing governor of New York and New Jersey (1702–1708). An oil portrait of Lord Cornbury by Arthur D. Pierce, titled *A Governor in Skirts*, shows Hyde in a dress. According to Katz in *Gay American History*, "A large portrait of Hyde, in a bright blue, low-necked dress and white gloves, is sometimes on exhibit at the New York Historical Society; it is quite a sight." (Courtesy Reed R. Apaghian.)

Memorial Hall was designed by architect H.J. Sahwarzman as a permanent memorial of the centennial year of American independence and served as a major draw to the centennial exposition. Bayard Taylor, an internationally renowned gay poet and writer, was asked by the Centennial Commission in Philadelphia to write the national hymn for the celebration. Taylor was the only gay person that we know of today who played such a major role in the nation's 100th birthday, but sadly his fame and reputation have since vanished. (Courtesy Philadelphia Historical Commission.)

Metropolitan Opera House
Philadelphia

PAVLOWA BALLET, Inc.

MAX RABINOFF, Managing Director

PRESENTS THE INCOMPARABLE

ANNA PAVLOWA

AND ENTIRE

RUSSIAN BALLET AND
SYMPHONY ORCHESTRA

MONDAY, NOVEMBER 23, 1914

The long association between opera and homosexuality can be traced to the castrato, as well as the historical prohibitions against women on the stage. In his book *The Queen's Throat: Opera, Homosexuality and the Mystery of Desire,* Waybe Koestenbaum draws parallels between opera divas and their fascination for gay men. Though Koestenbaum's book was praised by Susan Sontag, *Harvard Review* book critic Athena Andreadis took Koestenbaum to task. "It is the inevitable decline and fall of a diva—the increasingly pathetic comebacks—rather then her talent, that seem to claim the particular adoration of her gay fans. There is pathos and grandeur in the idol/devotee configuration, but also fathomless depths of self-hatred and contempt for the idealized female; such fixations have always disempowered women." On April 15, 1886, on the 21st anniversary of the assassination of President Lincoln, poet Walt Whitman lectured at the Opera House of Philadelphia. Jerome Loving, author of *Walt Whitman, The Song of Himself,* writes: "The Philadelphia Press described Whitman's voice as strong. Before he began, he noted objections to reviving bitter memories of the war and said he hoped to his dying day to gather with friends every April to remember Lincoln. Afterward, during an informal reception backstage, an impulsive young woman gave the bard 'a rousing smack on the lips.'" (Courtesy Reed R. Apaghian.)

PLAYS AND PLAYERS

OF THE
LEADING THEATRES IN PHILADELPHIA

Before and after Theatre
Don't fail to visit the

Hotel Walton

PALM ROOM

It's a delight to hear
PASCAL PARENTE
and his famous string quintette
direct from HOTEL SAVOY, London,
England, and the Restaurant Julien
of Paris

SPECIAL   SUNDAY   EVENING
CONCERTS

Main Foyer 6.30 to 9.30 P. M.

Lukes & Zahn

Proprietors

Published by
NIRDLINGER & WETHERILL
804
WALNUT ST.

Designed and Engraved by
GATCHEL & MANNING
N. E. Cor. 6th
& CHESTNUT STS.

The Plays and Players playbill was an umbrella publication that listed information about many of the theaters in Philadelphia. Plays and Players theater, at 17th and DeLancey Streets, was known as the Little Theater when it was built in 1911. The murals in the interior of the theater were painted by Edith Emerson, a protégé of Violet Oakley, a lesbian who had painted the exquisite murals in the Pennsylvania state capitol building. (Courtesy Reed R. Apaghian.)

Actress Gloria Swanson (1899–1983), autograph book and pen in hand, pretends to be a sales clerk in this 1920s photograph taken on the main floor of John Wanamaker's department store in downtown Philadelphia. Practicing to be a salesgirl for a role in a film, Swanson mingles with real employees as curious customers observe the goings-on. Wanamaker's began on the corner of Sixth and Market Streets on the former site of the house of George Washington when he was president of the United States. In time the building became known as Oak Hall, a men's clothing store that marked the beginning of John Wanamaker's career. In 1876, the store moved to 13th and Market Streets and was called the Grand Depot. In 1902, the store was expanded dramatically, making it the largest department store in the world.

Generations of Philadelphia gay men worked at Wanamaker's as retail sales clerks, managers, and display artists. Wanamaker's legacy as a magnet for gay men was known throughout the city. John Wanamaker, despite his enterprising business spirit, was no friend of homosexuals. At the beginning of the 20th century, he forbade the sale of *Leaves of Grass* in the Wanamaker bookstore because of Whitman's (same sex) "immorality." (Courtesy Reed R. Apaghian.)

In the 1800s, men were often photographed with their best friends, much like the photographs of Walt Whitman with his male companions or comrades. This photograph was found in the Cushman collection, an indication that these men were either friends of visiting actresses or perhaps involved in early Philadelphia theater. Their sexual orientation is unknown, but whether they were friends or brothers, gay or straight, affectionate same sex "couplings" in front of the camera was the order of the day. (Courtesy Reed R. Apaghian.)

This brochure advertising a circus on the John Wanamaker department store lot, at 15th and Chestnut Streets, probably attracted the attention of Walt Whitman. Some years earlier, the unemployed poet had become caught up in the hoopla of the P.T. Barnum Circus. Whitman, according to biographer Jerome Loving, had interviewed Barnum for the *Brooklyn Eagle* in 1846, "when the carnivalist and entrepreneur had just returned from Europe, having established the tiny General Tom Thumb. When Whitman asked him whether he had seen anything in the Old World that made 'him love Yankeedom less,' Barnum replied, his eyes flashing: 'My God! . . . no! Not a bit of it! Why, sir, you can't imagine the difference. There everything is frozen—kings and things—formal, but absolutely frozen; here it is life." (Courtesy Reed R. Apaghian.)

Part I.---Will conclude with a grand

ENCHANTMENT BALLET!

M'lle JOSEPHINE STOKES, premiere danseuse.

M'lles SMUCKER, NEIDE, and ANSTICE, Coryphees.

Les Nymphes Dansantes, M'lles STOUT, PRITCHETT, and COCHRAN.

Part II.

MUSIC—" Oft in the STILLY night."

GRAND FARCE in one act, by Gen'l BUTLER, entitled

THE SPOONY!!

Dramatis personae :

BONNY, the Spoony.	POMP, a Noble African.
WILLIAM, his G(U)EST.	BILLY, the Bretzel-man.

MUSIC—"Witches Incantation," from MACBETHELROY.

GRAND PROPHETIC) (BONNY NELL, (the wonderful Egyptian En-
PHANTASMAGORIA.) (chantress and Fortune-Teller.)

MUSIC—"A Parallax, a Parallax, a most confounded Parallax."

FEEDING OF THE ANIMALS, by JAMES STUART, the Pretender.
(Dick's son.)

MUSIC—" S————on a bob-tailed Mule." . Chorus.
(In which the audience are respectfully requested to join.)

When John Wanamaker's was dedicated at the close of its jubilee year on December 30, 1911, the Grand Court was the scene of many ceremonies. Federal, state, and city officials, foreign ambassadors, and wealthy bankers assisted then Mayor Blankenburg in welcoming Pres. William Howard Taft, who made the dedicatory address. As a 500-voice chorus sang two songs, the city reveled in new-found glory. Wanamaker's not only had the largest organ in the world—13 freight cars were needed to transport it to Philadelphia from the St. Louis 1904 Exposition, where it was purchased—it was also the first store in America to build a wireless tower and to have its own radio station, WOO. Just several blocks away from the melodies of military bands and congratulatory banners, homosexual Turkish bathhouses let loose their special brand of cheers and revelry. (Courtesy Dorothy C. Nickels.)

A FRIENDLY GUIDE BOOK *to*
PHILADELPHIA
and THE WANAMAKER *Store*

This view of Rittenhouse Square in the winter of 1921 gives no hint of the activity going on. Marc Stein, in *City of Sisterly and Brotherly Love*, writes, "Rittenhouse Square's popularity [as a popular cruising area] predated World War II . . . ," a claim substantiated by many gay men of the era. (Courtesy Philadelphia Historical Society.)

Henri David, Philadelphia's legendary jeweler and drag impresario, found the following letter tucked away in the floorboards of his new house at 1331 Pine Street. The letter was mailed from Atlantic City on September 16, 1924, to a Mr. Thomas A. Sherman Jr., in care of Frank Meehan at 13th and Pine Streets. (Courtesy Henri David.)

Tuesday afternoon

Dearest Tommie—lad!

Your letter was darlin' but am so sorry that your Mother has adopted that attitude towards me. If she would only let me explain to her that I'm not going to run away with her big son——at least not for four (4) years.

Dear, don't think you had better do as your family requested and not ever see me? Please say no. Please know that I love you more than anything in the world, but can't have you wreck your future for me. You understand! But, Tommie, if I don't see you every week as we planned I don't know *your Mothers prejudice make any difference. I only hope and pray it won't.*

Had a date with Frank Zito last nite. We went to dance and then the "La Vic." He thinks your fine and he was very nice. Today Ernie, Frank, Andre and the Call boys had luncheon here. Then Ray Dawson and Bill (whatever his last name is) came around and they have been singing and playing the banjo. Andre brought his good one around. It's stunning. Frank fixed the victrola and now we have music again. I think Andre may go up to town with me on Thursday. Tommie-lad will I see you on Thursday? Can I call or something. You see, I'm not positive as to where I shall be but may be able to let you know in my next letter. Remember this dear one! I love you and only you and will love you forever and wait that long if I must. Please love me a little and don't be blue. Be good and study hard. Forever my sincere love "El"

how I'll survive the winter. I want you every minute of the day and so I must see you at least once a week to appease that longing. And, dear you know I'd wait forever for you. Ten years aren't many and if you love me that's all I want. Please don't let your Mother's prejudice make any difference. I only hope and pray it won't.

Had a date with Frank Zito last nite. We went to dance and then the "La Vic." He thinks your [sic] fine and he is very nice. Today Ernie, Frank, Andre and the Call boys had luncheon here. Then Ray Dawson and Bill (whatever his last name is) came around and they have been singing and playing the banjo. Andre brought his good one around. It's stunning. Frank fixed the victrola and now we have music again. I think Andre may go up to town with me on Thursday. Tommie-lad will I see you on Thursday? Can I call or something. You see, I'm not positive as to where I shall be but may be able to let you know in my next letter. Remember this dear one! I love you and only you and will love you forever and wait that long if I must. Please love me a little and don't be blue. Be good and study hard. Forever my sincere love, "El"

Venture Inn

255 South Camac St.

Philadelphia 7, Pa.

"*Fair Philadelphia next is rising seen, betwixt two rivers, placed two miles between!*"

WILLIAM PENN

The Venture Inn, on South Camac Street, became predominantly gay in the 1940s. It is one of the oldest gay bars and restaurants in Philadelphia. The Venture Inn once served as a stable for the carriages of wealthy Philadelphians. It is one of the few surviving inns and taverns built as early as 1670. Named after Turner Camac, a wealthy Irish landowner who came to Philadelphia in 1804, the street began as a quaint thoroughfare. Early-American homes with tiny gardens lined the street at least until 1880. The city took an active role in transforming the street in the 20th century after a long period of decline, and the Poor Richard Club took the lead in beginning the renascence. Soon the area had the aura "of bohemianism of the Greenwich Village type," with literary, sketch, and yachtsman clubs dotting the landscape. During the police raids on gay bars in the 1940s and 1950s, the Venture Inn was spared because some of its clientele was heterosexual, attracted by the inn's huge vaudeville stage, where today there is a first-class restaurant. (Courtesy Venture Inn.)

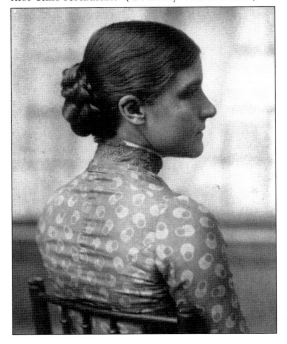

M. Carey Thomas (1844–1922), second president of Bryn Mawr College, hosted a visit by philosopher Bertrand Russell and his wife in 1896. Russell noted at that time Thomas's immense energy and the fact that she was generally feared by most at the college. Gertrude Stein used Thomas's romantic life—her relationship with a woman who in turn was involved with a man—in her short novel *Fernhurst.* (Courtesy Bryn Mawr College; photograph by Frederick Hollyer.)

Born in 1918, poet and author Lorraine Walker Bardsley, pictured here with a Philadelphia friend *c.* 1948, lived and worked in various parts of Philadelphia until her move to a reclusive farmhouse in Bucks County. In her 1999 memoir *Bittersweet*, Bardsley writes that her awakening as a lesbian took place in 1933. "Entering her yard," she writes, "I reached the shelter of evergreen trees fronting the house. Stealthily, I climbed the closest tree, reaching the roof of a lower porch. From there it was easy to step through a window into the bedroom of my beloved." In college, Bardsley dated men and went steady, though she said that the conflict of identity began to weigh heavily on her. Social pressures to marry forced her to change her life but on the eve of her honeymoon, she thought, "God help me, what have I done? My emotional life is with women, not with this man, so strange to me . . ." Eventually Bardsley came out and began to explore the closet days of the 1950s when Philadelphia police raided gay bars and conducted random body searches. "This whole new world of homosexuals with its butch and femme terminology," she writes, "was an exciting experience. The feeling of belonging was heady for I no longer felt alone."

Lorraine Walker Bardsley, self-described "New Hampshire Dyke," writes in *Bittersweet* that, in the early 1960s, she traveled with three other women around the perimeter of the United States. "In nine weeks we covered 14,000 miles, tenting out all the way. Just think of it—four women in one car and one small tent! Once a week we took a motel room so we could launder our clothes and ourselves. Pretty close quarters and nerves grew raw at times. Nonetheless, we saw much and experienced some exciting episodes. We camped out in all the National Parks. Back then camping had not really caught on, and we were free of crowds. For one dollar we were allowed to stay four nights at a Yellowstone." (Courtesy Lorraine Walker Beardsley.)

Philadelphia's Rosenbach Museum and Library, at 2010 DeLancey Place, contains one of the best gay and lesbian literature and history collections on the East Coast. As a museum brochure states, the collection includes "items related to the modern gay and lesbian experience as well as works by writers and artists who are generally acknowledged to have been gay, lesbian, or bisexual." The collection contains the handwritten manuscripts of Oscar Wilde and many other works. (Courtesy Philadelphia Historical Commission; photography by George E. Thomas.)

Bayard Taylor was born on January 11, 1825, in Kennett Square. He finished his schooling in 1842, and he decided to become a painter. He apprenticed under Henry E. Evans in West Chester and wrote poetry in his spare time. He left Evans's tutelage for a trip to Europe in lieu of a university education. The publication of his first book of poems, *Ximena; or, the Battle of Sierra Morena, and Other Poems*, predated the publication of his travel essays in the *Saturday Evening Post*. He became engaged to his high school sweetheart, Mary S. Agnew. The long engagement ended when she became sick with tuberculosis. They two were married for a mere two months before she died in December 1850. With the publication of *Joseph and His Friend*, known as the first American gay novel, which was serialized in 1869 by the *Atlantic Monthly*, Taylor was called "the most outspoken advocate of 'the other [homosexual] love' in mid-century America." At his death on December 19, 1878, Taylor had published some 50 books and at least 700 newspaper and magazine articles. (Courtesy Joseph A. Lordi and the Bayard Taylor Memorial Library.)

Lorraine Bardsley writes that in 1940 in a town just outside of Philadelphia she found Nell, "a young woman from the deep south of Mississippi." With music as the focus, the two women began a conversation. "She was studying to be a concert singer, and with a four-octane vocal range, was well on her way to success." After an intense affair at the end of World War II, Beardsley writes that her dream of a lifetime spent with Nell and her music came to an abrupt end. "A man had entered the scene, courted her, and won her over to marriage with him. The most painful time of all for me was when I acceded to Nell's request that I act as maid-of-honor in her wedding. This truly rubbed alt in the wound already excruciatingly deep." (Courtesy Lorraine Walker Bardsley.)

The Empress of the Blues, as Bessie Smith came to be called, lived for a while on Philadelphia's Kater Street—in what is now this hollowed-out and abandoned building—an association that helped her earn the title Philadelphia's Favorite Daughter. Born in 1898 in Tennessee, Smith met Ma Rainey, the Mother of the Blues, in 1926. An unfounded rumor was that Ma Rainey initiated Smith into lesbianism. Smith's later love affair with chorus girl Lillian Simpson forced her to endure the oppression of an abusive, playboy husband who beat her whenever he discovered her lesbian affairs. (Courtesy *Philadelphia Tribune*.)

Born in 1901 in Philadelphia to Henry Sr. and Frances McIlhenny, young Henry McIlhenny, thanks to his family's wealth, rubbed shoulders with the time-honored elite of Philadelphia. While at Harvard, McIlhenny decorated his rooms with drawings by Seurat and Matisse and afterwards collected paintings by David, Ingres, Cezanne, Renoir, Degas, Toulouse-Lautrec, and Picasso. He purchased his family's 1914 town house in 1951 and soon devoted all his time to collecting. "Never did it occur to him to live in any other city than the one in which he had been brought up," writes James Lord in his memoir, *A Gift for Admiration*. "Nor did it ever occur to him that he need be assiduously secretive about the reason which made it unthinkable that he should marry. If people knew—and everybody did—they were welcome to take it amiss, but when he gave parties for Princess Margaret, Brooke Astor, or Tennessee Williams, they set aside prejudice and hurried to attend if invited." McIlhenny was a member of the curatorial staff of the Philadelphia Museum of Art in the Department of Decorative Arts. His last great acquisition for the museum was van Gogh's *Rain*. McIlhenny died on May 12, 1986. (Courtesy Philadelphia Historical Commission.)

Arlene Sullivan (left) realized she was gay at age 18. She was at the peak of her teenage celebrity when this photograph was taken of her on stage as a regular dancer on *American Bandstand*, with emcee Gene Kaye (center) and another regular. Sullivan recalls that the events were so popular that Horn could get anyone to perform there. Although shy, Sullivan became quite outgoing when appearing on the show. When she discovered that most of the boys who danced on *American Bandstand* were gay, she said she was initially shocked but in the end wound up "really liking them." During a trip to New York to be photographed for *Sixteen* magazine, Sullivan recalls that she spent the days with the gay magazine photographer walking around Greenwich Village and then rushed back at the last minute to take the magazine photograph. (Courtesy Arlene Sullivan.)

Arlene Sullivan is photographed with *American Bandstand* boyfriend Kenny Rossi. From 1957 to 1960, Sullivan danced at *American Bandstand* studios at 46th and Market Streets. Invited by a regular to come on the show, she soon attracted fan mail and in no time became one of the most popular regulars herself, appearing on the cover of *Sixteen* and *Teen* magazines. Sullivan realized she was gay at 18 but liked boys for a time and said that Kenny Rossi was the only boy she really loved. Many of the regulars on the show were gay. "I was Catholic. I grew up in a Catholic Irish/Italian neighborhood, where there were lots of police officers, lots of firemen. It was a nice group. I had a lot of friends in the neighborhood but no one that I grew up with was gay, or at least we weren't aware of it at that time." (Courtesy Arlene Sullivan.)

On a July afternoon in 1965, the Adelphia Hotel, at 1229 Chestnut Street, looks like the epitome of tranquility; however, in its heyday in the 1920s, this popular Center City hotel housed out-of-town movie stars and celebrities. In 1928, the Adelphia advertised itself as a place where "Other Interesting People Lunch-Dine-Dance," with its tearoom, coffee grill, main dining room, and roof garden. By the 1980s, the hotel had become an apartment complex. (Courtesy Philadelphia Historical Commission.)

Feeding one another cherries and olives, Tyrone Smith (right)—the first and only president of Unity, an African American organization devoted to support those with HIV/AIDS—and his date celebrate Halloween in the mid-1960s. Smith remembers that "the guys would get dressed up in suits. Now you have drag queens all dressed up and their dates have their jeans hanging off their asses . . . back in those days if a man went out with you he was an enhancement . . . there was a sense of style . . ."

The independent and strong-willed Smith came out early both as a gay man and a drag queen. "At 26, I had had my first love affair that had gone sour. I didn't want to go back home. I wanted to keep my independence. Drag wasn't about soliciting or anything like that. It was about giving the illusion about being a woman. It was fun and creative. I never had a woman's name. I was always Miss Tyrone or Miss Smith . . ." (Courtesy Tyrone Smith.)

Gay Philadelphia activist Tyrone Smith (center) hosted many house parties at his first apartment at 17th Street and Lehigh Avenue. Many gay and non-gay African Americans hosted similar parties in the 1940s, 1950s, and 1960s in order to escape the racism prevalent in Center City bars and nightclubs.

The author (right) is shown immediately after high school graduation with his first and only girlfriend, Christine Arentz. In the 1960s, high school students often joked about "homos." Virulent homophobia did not exist at Great Valley Senior High School, although several male teachers were often whispered about.

On January 14, 1967

S E I
Presents
THE MISS NATIONALS
The Camp "MISS AMERICA"
The Nation's Most Beautiful Female Impersonators
MC'ed by Sabrina
The World's Most Masterful Mistress of Ceremonies

FOR QUICK SERVICE WRITE TO
BOX # 2130
PHILA., PA. 19103

The whole point of Camp is to dethrone the serious. Camp is playful, anti-serious. More precisely, Camp involves a new, more complex relation to 'the serious.' One can be serious about the frivolous, frivolous about the serious.

—Susan Sontag

Posters advertised drag beauty contests were a staple of 13th Street life in the late 1950s and 1960s. This one advertising the Miss Nationals (or the Camp Miss America) was sponsored by Sabrina Enterprises Inc. The Hotel Philadelphia, at Broad and Vine Streets (now demolished), was also the site of the annual Miss Philadelphia contest. The contest was organized by Jack Doroshow (Sabrina) (upper left), Henri David, and Jack Venuti. The big winner in the 1967 nationals was Harlow (Richard Finocchio). Harlow became the star of Frank Simon's 1968 film *The Queen*. Sometime in the 1970s, Harlow had a sex-change operation and became Rachel Harlow. (Courtesy Henri David.)

On Atlantic City's gay beach, 17-year-old Henri David is sitting pretty. In the 1960s, at the opening of the season and the gay beach, Henri David and his entourage would stage an opening performance. "This year I was carried onto the beach by musclemen. Every year I'd do something a little more outrageous," recalls David. Going swimming, however, since it messed up a boy's hair, was never a part of the seashore opening act. (Courtesy Henri David.)

Henri David's "drag mother," Sabrina (Jack Doroshow), was photographed in 1966. For most of gay Philadelphia in the 1960s, Sabrina was a mystery. Though he was not a part of the Center City nightlife, Sabrina hosted drag parties at his mansion. Henri David remembers, "He would hire a band, they'd serve booze . . . they were wild, wild parties. They eventually got raided and they made the news. But the kids were all thrilled because it was like a dream to go to this mansion with a circular driveway, a butler, and the whole nine yards. It was so decadent. Sabrina's mother took the money at the door. [He] actually looked like [David's] mother when he was in drag. [She] always wore black velvet and had blond hair, [and] would stand at the door and say, 'Hello darling, two dollars . . .' It was a surreal time in our lives. The parties would go on all night. We would rent school buses and bring whole crowds out from downtown . . . nobody had cars . . . we were kids." (Courtesy Mel Heifetz.)

Jack Doroshow (Sabrina) is shown in Center City c. 1966. By the 1960s, the idea had been suggested to Doroshow to host a Miss America-type drag pageant. (Courtesy Mel Heifetz.)

In the 1950s and 1960s, the place to go if you were gay and underage was Jimmy Neff's steakhouse, at Broad and Spruce Streets. Henri David (left) grasps the arm of Jimmy Neff while watching the Mummers Parade on Broad Street in 1960. "Jimmy Neff's steakhouse on New Year's Day was the place to be," said David. "You could get inside and look out the window and watch the parade from there. For those who couldn't get into the bars to get a drink to warm up, this was the other thing to do—go into Jimmy Neff's. It was always filled with drag queens and crazy people and it was wild. Neff was a straight man but extremely gay-friendly." (Courtesy Henri David.)

The Allegro Bar on Spruce Street near Broad was for years the best gay club in Philadelphia. James Mark Shrayer (left) was the original owner of the bar; a young Henri David holds the cat. Next door to the Allegro was the Mistique, a piano bar that attracted African Americanmusicians, jazz lovers, and a mixed cliental. Philadelphia pianist Beryl Booker, who played in Dizzy Gillespie's band and accompanied Billie Holiday on several tours, often played at the Mistique. The Mistique later became a lesbian bar. In the 1960s, the Allegro required male patrons to wear a jacket and tie. The dress code gradually disappeared and, by 1970, the bar was a democratic whirlwind of old and young, working class, suburban, and upper class. As the city's first mega-bar complex, the Allegro was three floors of nonstop action, including a piano bar and a dance floor. (Courtesy Henri David.)

"No drag queens in ladies room / No sex changes in men's room." read the makeshift signs on the bathroom doors at J & A Caterers in South Philadelphia during one of Henri David's innumerable drag balls in the early 1980s. Here, the iconoclastic David "meshes" with and mimics the rules. (Courtesy Henri David.)

"Give your tongue a sleigh ride!" and "Get yourself a tickle sickle!" were just two of the slogans shouted by Mike the ice-cream man on the gay beach in Atlantic City in the 1960s. Pictured here in July 1964, "the extremely gay-friendly Italian bull," would say, "Oh Mary," and sit on his ice-cream box, cross his legs, and act very gay. (Courtesy Henri David.)

This is an architectural rendering of an early 1950s drugstore on Philadelphia's Main Line by architect Thomas C. Nickels. In 1941, gay writer Christopher Isherwood, because of his work with the Quakers during World War II, spent some time on Philadelphia's Main Line. In his diaries, Isherwood notes that while taking the train out to Haverford station, "My first impression . . . was that all the people in the coach belonged to one of three or four distinctly recognizable families. Maybe this was only the contrast between relatively homogeneous Pennsylvania and the ever-changing polyglot population of Los Angeles. . . . The men were tall, bony, big shouldered, fair haired and quite nice looking, but somehow fatally 'pithed,' as though the marrow had been drained from their bones. They had an air of quiet anxiety. They spoke slowly, prudently, selecting their words from a small, odd vocabulary. The women were bright and energetic. They used no makeup, and their white skin was dotted with freckles. They had sandy gold hair, dragged back and twisted into a knot. The country we were passing couldn't possibly have been less 'my sort': it was tame, suburban, pretty, a landscape without secrets . . .'"

Carlton Willers, a native of Iowa, was 20 years old when, fresh from a stint in the U.S. Air Force, he landed a job as secretary to the curator of the picture collection at the New York Public Library, where he met famed artist Andy Warhol. This began a four-year love relationship with Warhol. Willers, who was attending Columbia University at the time and who eventually went to Warhol's alma mater Carnegie Mellon to teach, remembers accompanying Warhol to musicals and "wonderful theater things in the 1950s, when the whole world was different." Warhol had 18 cats at the time, all named Sam. They would roam the studio and sometimes knock over a bottle of India ink, Willers said. "Andy never got upset. His mother would come in with this big bucket and mop." (Courtesy Carlton Willers; photography by Trude Fleischmann.)

In 1963, Andy Warhol sketched Carlton Willers. Willers spent 30 years in New York and, for most of the time, he taught at Hunter College and operated an art gallery. He had moved to Philadelphia by the early 1980s. (Courtesy Carlton Willers.)

In the 1940s and 1950s, while Humphrey Bogart, Lauren Bacall, and Marlene Dietrich reigned supreme in Hollywood, Cleo, one of Philadelphia's most legendary drag queens, walked the streets of the city. Philadelphia then had many more gay clubs than it has today, and there were many straight bars that hosted drag nights, remembers Henri David. This photograph of Cleo, taken in Center City in 1962, plays down Cleo's outrageous taste in costumes that kept 1950s Mummers Parade organizers asking him back year after year. Cleo was in his 80s when he died in the 1970s. (Courtesy Henri David.)

Two
LIBERATION RISING

Those who make peaceful revolution impossible will make violent revolution inevitable.
—John F. Kennedy

Joan C. Meyers (right) and a friend relax in Meyers's massive 11th Street studio in 1967. A student at the Pennsylvania Academy of Fine Arts, Meyers described the studio on 11th Street as "our version of Andy Warhol's factory—it was huge, three floors of an old building, a big work space for us with all these films and picture-taking things I was doing. It was just a big lesbian playhouse." (Courtesy Joan C. Meyers.)

Essex Hemphill (1956–1995) lived with the parents of author Joe Beam to complete the anthology, *Brother to Brother: New Writings by Black Gay Men*. Seen here with Mrs. Beam, Essex is best known for his part in the films *Searching for Langston* and *Tongues Untied*. (Courtesy Lamont Steptoe.)

Anarchist Emma Goldman was the first person to advocate gay rights in America, though she was not a lesbian. In the early 1900s, Philadelphia police imprisoned her in the tower of city hall. Construction on Philadelphia's city hall began in 1893 and ended in 1901. This Second Empire French Renaissance Revival building is the tallest masonry building in the world, with 695 rooms, 250 sculptures, a subbasement, and a tower with 22-foot-thick walls. The "Tower of Philadelphia" was at different times in history used as a prison for Goldman and countless others. (Courtesy Archives/Library of the William Way Community Center.)

Philadelphia's Drake Hotel (now an apartment building), located west of Broad Street on Spruce Street, hosted many gay events beginning in the 1960s. In September 1963, the first conference of East Coast Homophile Organizations was held at the Drake Hotel. ECHO was the umbrella organization of many other similar groups based in New York and Washington. However, "After arrangements had been made to hold the event at the Adelphia, the hotel backed out just weeks before the convention," writes Marc Stein in *City of Sisterly and Brotherly Love* . . . A combination of legal action, negotiation, and violent threats made by Clark Polak of Janus, an early homophile rights organization for men and women, kept the conference at the Drake." In 1970, the Drake hosted Henri David's Miss Queen of Hearts Ball and Gay Halloween, a costume ball. Across the street from the Drake, Roscoe's, a gay bar of the 1970s and 1980s, was transformed into a low-fat yogurt shop in the 1990s. (Courtesy Philadelphia Historical Commission.)

Joan C. Meyers was photographed in her 11th Street studio in the late 1960s. On the weekends, Meyers and her friends would head to Rusty's, a popular lesbian bar near the TROC burlesque theater, at 10th and Arch Street, which had the paranoid atmosphere of a 1920s speakeasy. Rusty's and the nearby Variety Room went out of business in the early 1970s, when patrons tired of sneaking through back alleys to request admission through a peephole. (Courtesy Pat Hill; photography by Joan C. Meyers.)

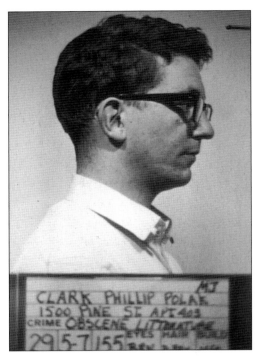

Drum Magazine publisher Clark Polak was once the most important and vocal gay activist in Philadelphia. In the early 1960s, he was elected president of the Janus Society, an early Philadelphia homophile organization that urged homosexuals of both sexes to adopt an irreproachable behavior code. Polak's controversial style won him friends and enemies alike. In 1965, Polak protested with 150 others when Dewey's restaurant on 17th Street refused to serve homosexuals and other nonconformist types. After enduring many years of harassment from city government over several other projects, he moved to California in 1970 and died in 1980. (Courtesy Archives / Library of the William Way Community Center.)

Marge McCann (left) and her then partner, Fran, enjoy the Atlantic City gay beach in the 1960s. In 1969, McCann ran unsuccessfully against Clark Polak for the presidency of Janus. The Mattachine Society, another early but more militant homosexual rights organization, was founded in 1950 by Harry Hay. In Los Angeles, Mattachine developed strategies for organizing a mass movement of homophile organizations. McCann favored a respectable militant approach in the fight for equal rights, whereas Polak was influenced by the sexual revolution and sexual liberation and channeled his protest energies into his magazine *Drum*. (Courtesy Marge McCann.)

These Philadelphia police officers, caught at a Henri David drag party in 1968 gazing at legendary drag queen Maralyn, call to mind Rainer Maria Rilke's comments on Cezanne: "He sat in front of it like a dog and simply looked, without any nervousness or ulterior motive." Drag queens were common in the Mummers Parades in the 1960s and 1970s, when gay and straight men of every size and shape would prance or clown up Broad Street on New Year's Day. Drag queens, in fact, were the one thing about the Mummers that always added an element of surprise and fun. Today's Mummers is a mostly a sanitized spectacle geared to (G-rated) television audiences and the awarding of prizes. (Photography by Joan C. Meyers.)

Philadelphian Joyce Finkelman might be preparing to rewrite Sappho's poetry at this Center City "toga" party in 1970. (Photography by Joan C. Meyers.)

Joan C. Meyers (left) lets out a 1969 New Year's Day wallop on Broad Street with friends Gina and George Tyler. Recalling life at Rusty's, Meyers said that among the staff there was Bee, "a miserable little thing who ran the bar and who took over after Rusty left." Meyers compared her to a nasty prison matron while Rusty "was like a retired sergeant from the Marines." (Photography by Joan C. Meyers.)

Award-winning composer and lyricist Tom Weinberg (fifth from the left) performs with his straight University of Pennsylvania classmates at Philadelphia's Mask & Wig Club c. 1969. Weinberg's out musical comedy Ten Percent Revue had a successful run in 1988. His albums of original songs include Gay Name Game and All American Boy. Gay Name Game (1979) was the first album of out, gay lyrics in the nation. At one point, the Mask & Wig Club closed its doors to all gay groups because it objected to posters for lesbian dances with the name Mask & Wig on them. (Courtesy Tom Weinberg.)

Richard Finochio was one of the stars of Frank Simon's 1968 film *The Queen*, a behind-the-scenes look at the drag Miss All America Beauty Pageant of 1967. Prior to the 1967 pageant, Finochio, who was known as Harlow, was a staple of drag contests and especially of the Miss Philadelphia contest organized by Henri David, Jack Doroshow (Sabrina), and Joe Venuti. (Courtesy Henri David.)

This photograph was taken inside the Humoresque, at 2036 Sansom Street. The 40-seat coffee shop attracted an eclectic crowd of poetry lovers and early beatniks, including interracial couples and gays and lesbians. Owner Mel Heifetz eventually sold the Humoresque when business slowed. "At its peak on a slow night it took in about $15. On a busy night we took in $70 to $80 and, over the whole week, I may have taken in about $250. I had to pay a salary, pay the rent. It never made any money, but it was about being young. It was about being in the center of what was happening," Heifetz said.

This group of men rings in 1964 on the corner of Broad and Spruce Streets as rain pelts marching Mummers and the soft pretzel man carries his wares through the gay assembly. Five years before Stonewall, there were very few opportunities for gay men to safely assemble in public to camp it up and be out. New Year's was a notable exception, especially in 1964 when the Mummers was less a corporate entity and more of an all-day circus with hundreds of drag queens—and other rustic surprises—on parade. (Courtesy Henri David.)

Another gathering takes place on Atlantic City's gay beach in 1964. (Courtesy Henri David.)

Kiyoshi Kuromiya (1943–2000), a national leader of the AIDS movement for many years and a person with AIDS, appears as a young teenager in Rittenhouse Square. Kuromiya founded the Critical Path Project, which included an Internet service that provided free access for persons with AIDS. Frank Leib, a friend of Kuromiya's in the 1970s, recalls that on the first day of class at Kuromiya's Free University course in mysticism at the University of Pennsylvania, the future AIDS activist handed out LSD tablets. Kuromiya also taught a gay liberation course, with Leib, at the University of Pennsylvania. (Courtesy Henri David.)

The glory days of Philadelphia's Electric Factory, the city's rock-'n'-roll concert palace before the capitulation of rock music to corporate interests, attracted the likes of Henri David. This photograph of David was taken by a club entertainer during the summer of 1969. (Courtesy Henri David.)

The infamous Zane, being outrageously gay on Atlantic City's gay beach in 1964, turns heads as far as the eye can see. (Courtesy Henri David.)

Richard Finochio (Harlow) is shown *c.* 1967 before his sex-change operation. Finochio's role in the 1968 *The Queen* brought him national attention. The photograph was taken at the 1967 Miss All American Beauty Pageant, which Raymond Murray in *Images in the Dark* described as, "a glamorous, sensational affair which gives center stage to these beauties, especially Philadelphia's Harlow, a willowy blonde waif with a mysterious and vulnerable air. After the crowning of the new queen, many of the attitude-throwing, jealous losers bare their sharp claws and venomous tongues, bitching about the winner and her oh-so-tacky dress!"

Maralyn (right) the famous drag queen from the 1940s and 1950s, used to throw her wig in a paper bag, shake it up, and then put it on her head. Although she never looked glamorous, she was certainly a lot of fun. Maralyn is shown with actress Elizabeth Coffey, who was once a boy named Phillip. Coffey starred in John Waters's films *Female Trouble* and *Pink Flamingos*. (Courtesy Henri David.)

Standing with friends and supporters c. 1974 in Washington Square are Pat Hill (second from the left) and Dan Sherbo (third from the left), cofounder of the bookstore Giovanni's Room. (Courtesy Arleen Olshan.)

Arleen Olshan (left) and Barbara, both members of Radical Lesbians in the 1970s, take a breather from a citywide Women's Day celebration in Rittenhouse Square. Olshan teamed up with Ed Hermance in the early 1970s to help build the Gay and Lesbian Community Center on Kater Street and was the center's first coordinator. When Pat Hill (owner of Giovanni's Room bookstore) put the store up for sale, Olshan and Ed Hermance purchased the business and moved Giovanni's to 1426 Spruce Street. "We were at this address for a year or two," Olshan says. "That building had been up for sale and when the new owner took it over they thought that we had been responsible for having turned Spruce Street into a big gay block and they thought of us as an undesirable business in their building." (Courtesy *Au Courant*; William Way Archives; photography by Susan Kurtz.)

Henri David and friends stroll the Atlantic City boardwalk on July 4, 1966. (Courtesy Mel Heifetz.)

Mable Red Top has been a well-known and popular Philadelphia drag performer since the late 1960s. Shown navigating Center City streets on crutches, Mable is currently affiliated with Club Key West on Juniper Street. (Courtesy Henri David.)

Private, gay African American house parties often included lesbians, although this party celebrating the 1964 Penn Relays does not show a mixed group. (Courtesy Tyrone Smith.)

Original members of Pudenda, a West Philadelphia women's collective at 3300 Hamilton Street, were a mixture of gay and straight, working women, and women in school. "It was open, anyone who needed a place to stay could live there. Eventually we had something like 15 women living in the house. People used to come to the house to come out. They knew it was a dyke house, they knew it would be accepting. We had wonderful times around the dining room table. We shared chores and cooked for one another. It was the healthiest way to come out," Arleee Olshan (second from the right) remembers. (Courtesy Arleen Olshan.)

Henri David (left), Joyce Finkelman, and an unidentified warrior spontaneously struck this pose at Joan Meyers's studio in 1968. The photograph might be said to symbolize the shedding of masks or the closet, though this November 1968 photograph was taken one year before the Stonewall riots in New York. The hand-held artillery, as well as the militarism of the helmets and horn, calls to mind Plato's admonition that "An army of lovers cannot lose. The love of one man for another—more than any other form of love, Plato thought—fills individuals with the spirit of freedom and defiance," Frank B. Leib, a Philadelphian, wrote in his 1999 book *Fierce Companions*, "For this reason, tyrannical governments inevitably persecute it: 'I know there are some people who call [male love] shameless,' Plato admitted, 'but they are wrong. It is not immodesty that leads them to such pleasures, but daring, fortitude, and masculinity—the very virtues which [men] recognize and welcome in their [male] lovers.'" (Photography by Joan C. Meyers.)

Barbara Gittings (left) stands alongside the Homophile Acton League (HAL) banner *c. 1970*. The Daughters of Bilitis (DOB), a lesbian organization founded in California in the 1950s, attracted lesbian newcomers after Philadelphia police raided Rusty's. In 1983, Ada Bello told the *Gay News* that the Philadelphia chapter of DOB later "voted unanimously to re-group under the name Homophile Action League." Bello told the newspaper that DOB felt the need to form an action-oriented group that included men. HAL worked to challenge the 1970 gubernatorial candidates on their stand on gay rights, held forums, testified before the state Republican and Democratic platform committees, and petitioned Philadelphia City Council for a gay rights bill. (Courtesy William Way Community Center.)

A founder of the Philadelphia Gay Liberation Front (GLF), Basil O'Brien dropped out of Goddard College and Temple University. O'Brien worked on an early gay newspaper, *Plane Dealer* (later the *Gay Dealer*), before he started to organize GLF meetings in an old warehouse south of Philadelphia's South Street, where participants sat on crates. Along with Frank Leib and Tom Ashe, O'Brien helped organize a consciousness-raising group at Houston Hall at the University of Pennsylvania; there the trio met Hal Tarr. Leib remembers that GLF included fewer than 10 members at this time. One of GLF's early projects was the disruption of a Catholic mass in 1970, when it became known that the pastor of a church was about to deliver a sermon on "the evils of homosexuality." Much to the surprise of the protesters, the priest turned out to be a kind old man. The party adjourned to the parish hall with people from the congregation who were interested in a friendly discussion; the people and the priest were very sympathetic. In 1972, O'Brien left Philadelphia for San Francisco, upset by the split between GLF and the Gay Activist Alliance. His involvement with the Pentecostal Holiness Church and gospel radio talk show host/commentator Louise Williams when he returned to Philadelphia eventually led to his becoming a virtual superstar in Philadelphia's black gospel community, where he had his own radio show. (Courtesy Suzanne O'Brien and Frank B. Leib.)

Looking casual in her new "gay liberation outfit," Barbara Gittings (left) holds one end of the Christopher Street Gay Liberation Day 1970 banner. The Christopher Street Gay Liberation Day festivities in New York had been planned to honor the rioting at the Stonewall Inn only one year before. In 1969, a resolution was passed that read: "That the Annual Reminder, in order to be more relevant, reach a greater number of people and encompass the idea and ideals of the larger struggle in which we are engaged. . . . We propose that a demonstration be held annually on the last Saturday in June in New York City to commemorate the 1969 spontaneous demonstration on Christopher Street . . ."

Swirls of light surround Pat Hill as she prepares to leave the 11th Street studio, or "the Barn," that she shared with Joan C. Meyers. Hill purchased Giovanni's Room bookstore in 1974 from bookstore founders Tom Weinberg, Bernie Boyle, and Dan Sherbo. Hill developed the bookstore and brought women's events such as Wine, Women, and Song and women's art and photography shows to the store. (Photography by Joan C. Meyers.)

Looking like an actress on the set of a 1960s Jean Luc Goddard film, Pat Hill recalls evenings at Rusty's, Philadelphia's premier lesbian bar in the 1960s and 1970s. Hill once wrote an article in *Wicca*, a lesbian separatist newsletter, about the bar's watered-down drinks and terrible service. She was barred from Rusty's but admits that she "snuck in one time on Halloween to dance, but I never took my mask off." (Photography by Joan C. Meyers.)

Joan peddled with all the strength her little legs had and Prudence held tight.

This cartoon by Joan C. Meyers illustrates what it is like to be part of an attractive all-woman couple in a jungle of predatory men bent on finding conventional mates.

Reed R. Apaghian, founder and owner of the Astral Plane restaurant, one of Philadelphia's most eclectic and memorable dining spots, poses like Count Dracula. Apaghian, a sometime actor, came to New Hope when he was 19 and got involved with Motion Picture Center East. He worked for the director (who also directed the *Bonanza* television series) as a carpenter and painter initially but was later cast as the lead in *The Gentle People and the Quiet Man*, a film about the life of an Amish youth. (Courtesy Reed R. Apaghian.)

Reed R Apaghian (left) not yet 16, clowns around with his first boyfriend *c.* 1960. (Courtesy Reed R. Apaghian.)

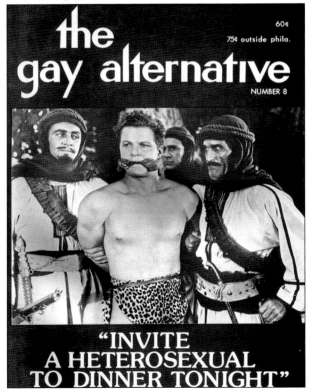

The Gay Alternative Collective had regular meetings on the University of Pennsylvania campus and in the homes of collective members. Issue No. 8, with Tarzan's Boy as the entrée of a cannibalistic barbecue, was every bit as eye-catching as issue No. 10, with its Oscar Wilde icon cover. Graphic artist Joe McGlone did the covers for many issues, and he relished the idea of presenting Wilde as a Russian saint. Gay Alternative members included Jeffrey Escoffier, Chuck Goldfarb, David Gordon, Matthew Grande, Rich Grzesiak, Ed Hermance, Phil Laird, Harry Langhorne, Steve Mirman, and Thom Nickels. (Courtesy Robert Schoenberg.)

A more formalized look at lesbian culture is expressed perfectly in Peggy Duffy's eyes in this exquisite photograph taken by Joan C. Meyers.

GAYZETTE

THE WEEKLY PHILADELPHIA GAYZETTE · 10¢

VOL. I. NO. 36   DECEMBER 20-27, 1974

COUNCIL HEARS TESTIMONY ON 1275; ARCHDIOCESE, POLICE OPPOSE BILL

by John Harkins

The Law and Government Committee of Philadelphia City Council held public hearings on Bill 1275 on Wednesday, December 18. The hearings were attended by approximately 100 proponents and 45 opponents of the bill.

Over 70 persons wished to testify, and less than half of these were heard on Wednesday. Chairperson Bellis said at the close of the session that the Committee would reconvene for additional testimony at a date to be announced later.

The Committee heard the unexpected opposition of the Archdiocese of Philadelphia and of the city's police and firefighters.

Principal Opposition

Father Charles McGrordy, Cardinal Krol's representative, denounced gays as "offering nothing positive to society and threatening those institutions which do benefit for society," the family and the home. He agreed with Bellis that society has had to deal with its prejudices against racial, religious and ethnic minorities , but said that gays differ from the norm in a more fundamental way which is contrary to the Judeo-Christian ethic.

Raymond M. Hemmert, president of the Firefighters Union of Philadelphia, explained that "team spirit" is necessary among firemen for their own survival. He said that the presence of gays would lead to the destruction of the mutual trust and respect required. The military refuses to accept gays, he said, so "why should we?"

John Quinn, of the Fraternal Order of Police, said that his men "should not have to work with deviates" and foresaw the corruption of children if the bill passes.

Deletion of Definition

Clarence Farmer, Chairperson of the Human Relations Commission which had re-
(Please turn to HEARINGS, page 4)

ANALYSIS

by Dan Martin

Wednesday's hearings on Bill 1275 leave much room for interpretation and speculation. Practically, the paramount question remains: How did the testimony affect the committee members(if at all); and will they read the bill out favorably or unfavorably to City Council? With no decision reached and the hearings scheduled to reconvene at an unspecified time next year, the answer to this question must be patiently awaited.

Although one must assume that the overriding issues involved are political, the testimony itself dealt with the social, moral, and legal implications of the bill. The most heatedly and repeatedly discussed issues were those of a social and moral nature.

Opponents of the bill expressed concern that civil rights for homosexuals would erode everything from the innocence of elementary school children to the very structure of our society.

Some parents called for the wrath of God to fall upon anyone who would further
(Please turn to ANALYSIS, page 3)

Season's Greetings

The *Weekly Gayzette* was founded and edited by singer/songwriter Tom Weinberg. The *Gayzette* staff included Dan Martin, Joe DeMarco (editor of *New Gay Life*), Rusel Silkey, Harry Langhorne, and Tommi Avicolli-Mecca. (Courtesy Tom Weinberg.)

The group Radical Queens, seen here in the 1973 Philadelphia Gay Pride Parade, was founded by Cei Bell and writer/activist Tommi Avicolli-Mecca in 1973. Radical Queens was originally a committee of the Gay Activist Alliance until it branched out on its own. (Courtesy William Way Archives and Library.)

In 1973, the board of the newly formed Eromin (Erotic Minorities) Center grins ear-to-ear. The 10th-anniversary Eromin resource guide stated that "Amid the turbulent social, political and cultural ferment of the late 1960s and early 1970s, the origins of the Eromin Center are to be found . . ." The center began as an outgrowth of the Philadelphia Gay Switchboard, a telephone counseling referral and information service. In the beginning, Eromin attracted grants from the New York-based Van Ameringen Foundation and the Philadelphia Foundation. In 1979, the center became an outpatient psychiatric clinic and offered training for human services providers. In 1989, it had a viable foster care program and a program for Cuban refugee minority youth. In 1982, Eromin was the only center certified as a state counseling service and the only one with programs for sexual minority youth in the nation. In the fall of 1983, the *Philadelphia Gay News* began a multipart series titled "Investigating the Eromin Controversy," by Victoria Brownworth. "Some call it 'Eromingate,'" Brownworth wrote, "to others it is more serious. At issue is the mismanagement and abuse of public monies . . . abuses that are punishable under law. . . . Eromin must not be destroyed or weakened. It must be cleaned out, rebuilt, and set on a responsible course that will ensure its growth and enduring usefulness." That never happened. Eromin eventually closed its doors for good. (Courtesy William Way Center.)

Looking like she has cycled into the heart of a Nevada desert, Roberta Hacker surveys the area near Front and Bainbridge Streets. Hacker's left arm had been broken in a previous motorcycle accident (discreetly hidden within the folds of her military jacket). In the 1970s, Hacker was involved with radical lesbians at the Women's Center at 46th and Chester Avenue. She also worked with Joan C. Meyers and Victoria Brownworth on the lesbian/feminist *Wicca*, a newspaper Hacker recalls as being "socio-political and nicely laid out." (Photography by Joan C. Meyers.)

Recalling the Age of Aquarius and the smell of patchouli oil, Jeffrey Escoffier (left) and Luke Fitzgerald give one another a gay liberation squeeze. Escoffier was a member of the Gay Alternative Collective, which published *Gay Alternative* magazine. In the November 10, 1975 issue, Escoffier penned a long essay on Oscar Wilde's politics, titled "The Homosexual As Artist As Socialist." This photograph was used for a 1973 cover of *Gay Alternative* magazine. (Photography by Joan C. Meyers.)

Sharky La Chance (left), born Sharyn M. La Bance (1949–1999), was a diva/dandy and self-admitted poker-faced list compiler who once began a semiautobiographical novella entitled *There's No Return, No Deposit.* She is shown with a young and sultry-looking Victoria Brownworth, an accomplished journalist, the author of eight books, and a Pulitzer Prize nominee. La Chance loved motorcycles, songs from *South Pacific* ("There Is Nothing like a Dame"), and making lists of her favorite things. (Photography by Joan C. Meyers.)

John Edgar (right) and his lover Michael Weltmann walk across a University of Pennsylvania playing field in 1978 for a game of softball. Edgar's passion for sports, especially softball, led to a lifetime involvement in the City of Brotherly Love Softball League (CBLSL). He and Weltmann were partners for seven years. Weltmann was the first openly gay man to speak before the United Nations. Weltmann's work in foster care—he started the first public adoption process in the United States for placing gay youth with gay couples—brought about this honor. (Courtesy John Edgar.)

A Philadelphia lesbian legend, writer Anita Cornwell has the distinction of being the author of the first collection of essays by an African American lesbian. *Black Lesbian in White America* was published by Naiad Press in 1983. She is also the author of several novels. Cornwell's short story "First Love and Other Sorrows" appeared in the November 9, 1975 issue of Philadelphia's *Gay Alternative*. Cornwell was honored in 2000 by the Annual Lambda Literary Festival, which was held in Philadelphia. (Courtesy NAIAD Press, with the permission of Anita Cornwell.)

This impromptu gathering probably took place after one of city's gay pride marches in the early 1970s. In the May 12, 1974 *Today* magazine cover story, writer Rod Townley wrote, "Homosexuals were once almost underground. Now they're becoming more and more visible, especially in Center City. And they're not apologizing as they demand that the Bill of Rights that was signed here nearly two centuries ago finally be applied to them, too . . . . Because so many homosexuals, both men and women, have been coming out of the closet in the last few years, there is an emerging public awareness of their existence. Suddenly there is a vast contingent of gays living in Philadelphia. They have always been here, but until recently, only the most flagrantly effeminate were recognized (and discriminated against) by the heterosexual majority. . . . Most 'straights' (heterosexuals) are by now aware that there are some gay bars in town. But few realize there are almost two dozen within a mile radius of City Hall . . ." (Courtesy William Way Archives/Gay Alternative Collection.)

Philadelphians Mary Ann Parsons (left) and Kate Valk are shown at Parsons's studio on Fourth Street *c.* 1974. (Photography by Joan C. Meyers.)

John Whyte (left) and Tom Weinberg, partners for many years, relax in a spacious bathtub. The couple, who met on a train platform at Philadelphia's 30th Street Station in 1973, have two children. The children live with their mothers in Boston but spend time with Whyte and Weinberg on the weekends. "The kids are terrific," Whyte told the author of *Men Together*, a 1998 Running Press book about male couples. "They're interesting and funny and out-of-control." Similarly, Weinberg talked about being a proud parent. (Courtesy Tom Weinberg.)

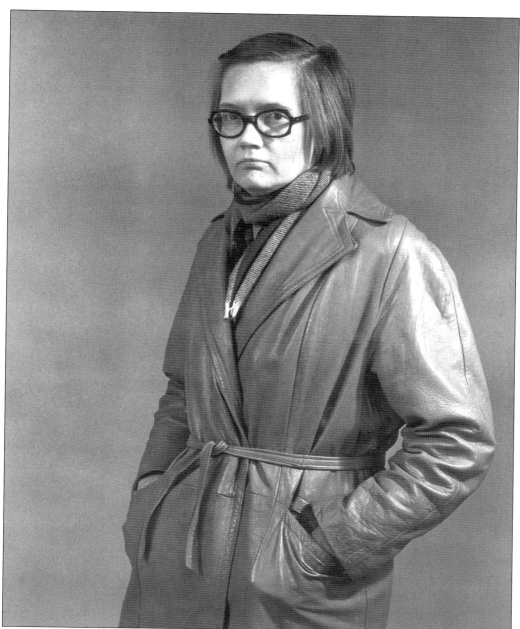

Nancy E. Krody of the United Church of Christ, shown in 1974, was one of the early pioneers of the Philadelphia gay/lesbian Christian movement. Krody, the coordinator of the Gay Caucus of the UCC, set up an information table in the 1970s when several hundred UCC ministers met at Ursinus College for their annual meeting. The information table was an important step for Krody, since she had announced her coming out several months before to the congregation of St. Paul's United Church of Christ in Springfield Township. The *Weekly Gayzette* reported that Krody planned to show the film *A Position of Faith*, the story of the ordination of gay 26-year-old gay William Johnson as a UCC pastor. (Photography by Joan C. Meyers.)

The personal and autobiographical themes of Michael Biello's 1978 "Two Men Dancing (Dances Around the Faggot Tree)" was a collaboration between Billo and Ishmael Houston-Jones (center). "Using props from the tree, the men try on roles. Poignantly, they wear blindfolds and touch. Before it is too late they see one another, and their improvisation . . . develops that growth," a dance critic reported. (Courtesy Dan Martin.)

Two men march together in Philadelphia's 1973 Gay Pride Parade. (Courtesy *Au Courant*.)

The magazine *New Gay Life*, founded and edited by Joe DeMarco, had a two-year publishing success in the late 1970s. The March 1978 edition included an interview with Ed Hermance and Arleen Olshan, fiction by Tommi Avicolli, and a column on sadism and masochism by Ken George. Virtue Records also advertised an appearance by singer Anthony Louis at the Metropolitan Community Church's Sunday 9:00 p.m. worship service. (Courtesy Robert Schoenberg.)

Dominic Rolla (center foreground) marches on the Benjamin Franklin Parkway in Philadelphia's second Gay Pride Parade. In a 1974 issue of *Today* magazine, Rolla characterized Philadelphia gay life at the time: "The 13th Street crowd is still into a dress-up kind of thing. Everything from fat heels and half-buttoned body shirts up to the full queen regalia. Effeminacy is admired much more in the gay community here than it is either in San Francisco or New York." (Courtesy *Au Courant*.)

The 1973 Gay Pride Parade stopped in front of Philadelphia's City Hall. Franny Price of Diversity of Pride has successfully coordinated Philadelphia's pride parades for many years. (Courtesy *Au Courant*.)

A young Juan David Acosta, poet and former executive director of Gay and Lesbian Latino AIDS Education Initiative, prepares to speak at a local event. (Courtesy William Way Archives and Library.)

Pat Hill (left) and Joan C. Meyers were a couple for more than seven years. Hill generated Philadelphia newspaper headlines in the mid-1970s when she brought a discrimination suit against the Philadelphia Department of Recreation, her employer for many years. Hill had left her position with the department to operate Giovanni's Room and to become more involved in the gay liberation movement. When she attempted to return to her job some years later, she was told there were no openings. Hill attempted to regain her old position by taking elementary civil service tests, in which she scored top marks but was repeatedly denied her job. She won the suit and was reinstated. (Photography by Joan C. Meyers.)

The Big Bambino, Mayor Frank Rizzo, was a towering hulk of a man. Tough, resilient, stubborn, and cut from a John Wayne mold, the mayor could also be charismatic and warm. In an interview conducted with him shortly before his death in the early 1990s, he spoke tenderly of a police officer friend dying of AIDS. As a former chief of police, however, officers under him routinely rounded up gay men. The author and a friend were taken into custody one summer night in 1974 while talking on a doorstep. Once inside the van we discovered 10 gay men all plucked from the sidewalk. As the van made its way to the city's roundhouse, or temporary jail, the driver would occasionally point to other men on the street perceived to be gay and, once again, the van would pull over. While he was mayor, police raided gay and lesbian clubs and closed coffeehouses.

Due to his ambivalence toward gays and lesbians, most in the community would not consider him a friend. He was charming, however, and could win over his staunchest enemies with his powerful personal charisma. During an interview with the author, Rizzo spoke in a style that he used to disarm his critics. He finished the interview with a friendly, "Anything you want to say about me you can say it, anything you want to add—no problem." (Courtesy William Way Archives and Library.)

ANTHONY LOUIS

Anthony Louis's song "Fantasy" originally contained the word "liberation," which raised some eyebrows in the industry because of a possible link to same-sex affection and gay liberation. Although there were plenty of concerts—over 300 college concerts in one year—Louis also appeared on the *David Frost Show*, the *Mike Douglas Show*, and the *Joey Bishop Show*, and had a number of album recording opportunities as well. Later, Louis was active in early gay politics and friendly with activists such as Tommi Avicolli-Mecca. (Courtesy Anthony Louis.)

"Puttin' It on at the Ritz" c. 1976 are, from left to right, Jim Harvey, Tyrone Smith, and Fred Thompson. One of the trademarks of the Ritz was its accessibility and lack of pretension. On warm nights the front door always remained open, so people passing on the sidewalk got a quick glimpse of the crowded and always animated bar. Currently there are no African American bars in Philadelphia in contrast to the several that existed years ago. (Courtesy Tyrone Smith.)

Three
PREPARING TO ASSIMILATE

Don't tell me peace has broken out, when I've just bought some new supplies.
—Bertolt Brecht

Joe Beam compiled a book while working at Giovanni's Room. "The most important contribution to African American gay culture from Philadelphia is *In the Life: A Black Gay Anthology*," said Ed Hermance of Giovanni's, a gay bookstore on the corner of South 12th and Pine Streets. Beam began a second anthology but was unable to complete it before his death from AIDS-related causes in 1988. (Courtesy Arleen Olshan.)

Appropriately posed in front of a bronzed torso of an ancient warrior is this 1975 group of gay and lesbian eagles. The photograph includes, from left to right, the following: (standing) Tom Weinberg, founder and editor of the *Philadelphia Gayzette*; Dennis Rubini, one-time head of the Gay Activist Alliance and teacher of a gay liberation course at Temple University; Shelden Reisen; Phillip Marra; Bryna Aronson, who worked with the American Civil Liberties Union; Mark Segal, founder of the Gay Raiders and the *Philadelphia Gay News*; and Barbara Gittings, longtime editor of the *Ladder*; (sitting) Tommi Avicolli-Mecca, founder of Radical Queens, local news editor and, later, editor in chief for the *Philadelphia Gay News*; and Harry Langhorne, early contributor to the *Gay Alternative*. In 1974, Dennis Rubini told the *Philadelphia Inquirer* that "Philadelphia is Greater Peyton Place. Everybody knows what everyone else is doing. This is good in that it creates some sense of community, bad in that it cuts down on the freedom to pursue variant life-styles." Rubini described Philadelphia as primarily a family city with "a densely monogamous atmosphere. Even the drag queens are conservative. Sure they dress wildly, but I assure you the dream of every drag queen in Philly is to be picked up in a fancy car by some rich, uptight gay and be taken out to his expensive home in the suburbs." (Courtesy Tom Weinberg.)

A thrift-store version of New York's Chelsea Hotel, Philadelphia's Parker Hotel, at 12th and Spruce Streets, has always had a gritty, offbeat ambiance. The hotel is located in the heart of Philadelphia's "gayborhood" and, in the 1970s, employed a not-so-gay-friendly staff. Inside the Parker was a restaurant and bar, which for many years offered cheap food, draft beer, and waitresses who called you "hon." The bar later became the Westbury, one of the city's more popular gay bars. (Courtesy Philadelphia Historical Commission.)

Ed Hermance, owner/manager of Giovanni's Room, stands among some of the store's 25,000-plus titles. From the store's humble beginning on South Street in 1973, Giovanni's has grown to become among the oldest and very best gay and lesbian bookstores in the country. The store hosts at least 40 or 50 author appearances a year. For years, Giovanni's outdoor signs and window displays have created an open street presence for lesbians and gay men, something rare for any city. "Crossing the store's threshold has had an extraordinary symbolic significance for hundreds, perhaps thousands of people coming out . . ." Hermance says. (Courtesy W. Way Community Center.)

John Cunningham (left) and Tommi Avicolli-Mecca appear at an early activist meeting. Cunningham coauthored *A Way of Love, a Way of Life: A Young Person's Guide to What It Means to Be Gay*. Avicolli-Mecca is the author of *Between Little Rock and a Hard Place* and a co-author of *Hey Paesan: Writing by Lesbians and Gay Men of Italian Descent*. (Courtesy William Way Archives and Library.)

Becky Birtha is the author of two volumes of short stories, *For Nights Like This One* and *Lovers' Choice*, and a collection of poetry, *Forbidden Poems*. Ed Hermance of Giovanni's Room said that Birtha's stories "have a vivid sense of place as well as an emotional depth rare among storytellers." (Courtesy Becky Birtha.)

A traffic light does not stop the high spirits and feelings of solidarity that seem to be running wild among these participants in Philadelphia's 1973 Gay Pride Parade. Big activist hair was the order of the day. (Courtesy *Au Courant.*)

Big hats, Coca Cola, sunglasses, and gay and lesbian liberation define this small 1973 Gay Pride entourage. (Courtesy William Way Archives and Library.)

You must also recognize the fact that homosexual periods, if I dare use the expression, are in no way periods of decadence. On the contrary, I do not think it would be inaccurate to say that the great periods when art flourished—the Greeks at the time of Pericles, the Romans in the century of Augustus, the English at the time of Shakespeare, the Italians at the time of the Renaissance, the French during the Renaissance and again under Louis XIII, the Persians at the time of Hafiz, etc., were the very times when homosexuality experienced itself most openly, and I would even say, officially. I would almost go so far to say that periods and countries without homosexuality are periods and countries without art.

—Andre Gide, *Corydon*

With her wand down in a ponderous time-out, Glenda, the good witch from Oz, gazes at someone or something in her left field of vision. Behind her, guarded curiosity and uncertainty color the faces of bystanders as Philadelphia's 1973 Gay Pride Parade makes it way down Benjamin Franklin Parkway. (Photography by Joan C. Meyers.)

"The telephone is the greatest nuisance among conveniences, the greatest convenience among nuisances," Robert Lynd once remarked. Lynd knew nothing of the Lesbian Hotline, a centralized information service for lesbians, dedicated to the elimination of nuisances. The March 1975 *Gayzette* stated, "Two and a half years ago, if a lesbian came to Philadelphia and wanted to find other lesbians, where could she go? It wasn't until a stranger came to town and questioned what services there were for lesbians that we realized how inadequate connections were in this city. She helped to organize a group of 20 women who were interested in the idea. The whole group got together for a weekend marathon, getting to know each other, sharing experiences, identifying the needs of lesbians in the city, and developing a way to fulfill them." (Photography by Joan C. Meyers.)

After 1971, the *Philadelphia Inquirer* won many Pultizer Prizes. Especially noteworthy was the series "America: What Went Wrong" by Pultizer Prize-winning investigative reporters Barlett and Steele in 1991. Although the newspaper continues to publish many progressive commentary pieces, the rise of so-called corporate journalism has put an end to much of the newspaper's derring-do. (Courtesy William Way Archives and Library.)

Bill "Woody" Wood celebrates a birthday at the now-defunct Steps bar. Wood, owner of Philadelphia's most popular gay bar, Woody's, began working in various gay bars such as Roscoe's on Spruce Street in the mid-1970s. His charitable contributions to the lesbian, gay, bisexual, and transgender community have been noteworthy. (Courtesy Mel Heifetz.)

The author (second from left) was a callow and naïve youth when this photograph was taken at 30th Street Station. He is on his way home to his (then) apartment in Boston with his sister Mary (left), his mother, Teresa (right), and his sister Carolyn (front).

The fountain in the background seems but another prop in this early public expression of gay pride. (Courtesy William Way Archives and Library.)

The Gay Activist Alliance, which split from Gay Liberation, was seen by some as more politically conservative than its predecessor. (Courtesy William Way Archives and Library.)

"Getting old in this country is no fun," says Mel Heifetz. "All of a sudden you start wearing that same cologne that all older men wear—it's called 'Invisible.' You are totally out of sight of everyone that's young and attractive, everybody that's interesting." Heifetz, however, is best known for his charitable giving. His gifts to AIDS groups since the 1980s such as the Homosexual Rights Campaign, American Civil Liberties Union, Gay, Lesbian, and Straight Education Network, and to television's *In the Life,* as well as numerous local charities have been significant enough to make him Philadelphia's most generous and most politically astute businessman. (Courtesy Mel Heifetz.)

Marge McCann (right) and a fellow actress ham it up on the set of the lesbian play *Last Summer at Blue Fish Cove.* The play, which had a successful run in 1986–1987 for many weeks at the Walnut Street Theater, was about a tragic death and the coming together of the community. "It was the first time I performed on stage since I was a Girl Scout," McCann said. (Courtesy Marge McCann.)

Good food kept simple and served with love was a daily occurrence at Mom's Restaurant at 1713 South Street. Mom's was opened in 1987 by Ardmore native Matt McClernon, a talented photographer and illustrator, and his partner Joe Quinn. Mom's quickly became a sensation, attracting a primarily gay and lesbian crowd during the week and a straight suburban crowd on the weekends. Mom's served only one entrée a night; for $10, diners got a complete dinner with appetizer, dessert, and coffee. Before opening Mom's, Quinn and McClernon operated the Salad Workshop on Long Beach Island, New Jersey. After McClernon's death in 1990 from AIDS-related causes, Quinn kept Mom's open for a year and a half. McClernon's obituary stated that the 36-year-old restaurant owner, "who made his patrons feel comfortable and his friends feel loved, died . . . of AIDS at his home in Center City . . ." It was the only the second time that an obituary in the *Philadelphia Inquirer* mentioned AIDS as the cause of death. Though McClernon wanted AIDS mentioned in his own obituary, this sort of honesty did not go over well with the patrons of Mom's in the early 1990s. "After Matt's death we experienced a surge of customers, but mostly these were people showing their support," said Quinn. "We lost our suburban weekend crowd completely and I eventually had to close." (Courtesy Joe Quinn.)

Matt McClernon (left) and Joe Quinn are shown with friend Nancy Powell in a supremely happy moment in Provincetown, Massachusetts. (Courtesy Joe Quinn.)

Joe Quinn (right) sold his car in 1979 and took out a $10,000 loan so that he and Matt McClernon could open the Salad Workshop. They later sold the business to open Mom's in 1987. Gerald Etter, a *Philadelphia Inquirer* food critic, commented: "If you sometimes tire of leafing through the menus, or if your brain balks now and then trying to choose between one dish or another, here's a home remedy: Try Mom's Homestyle Restaurant." McClernon and Quinn are shown on opening night. (Courtesy Joe Quinn.)

Sandy Beach, a well-known drag performer at Philadelphia's 12th Air Command bar, relaxes near Atlantic City's gay beach c. 1970. Beach got the name Sandy Beach from being a dolphin trainer in Atlantic City. When he came to Philadelphia in the mid-1980s, he performed with his group, the Salt Water Taffys at the DCA club. For a time, Beach opened for groups such as Robert Hazard and the Heroes. He went on to entertain "gay bingo crowds at the Sands in Atlantic City." (Courtesy Henri David; interview with Sandy Beach.)

The Penguin Place Community Center board relaxes after a heady early-1980s meeting in the apartment of William Way on 13th Street. Shown are, from left to right, the following: (front row) Walter Lear, unidentified, Michael Card, Steve Mirman, William Way, and Marge McCann; (back row) two unidentified persons, Ada Bello, and unidentified. (Courtesy Marge McCann.)

Knighted "Philadelphia's best known gay activist" by the *Philadelphia Inquirer* in 1974, Mark Segal is seen here chatting in his (once signature) toupee with controversial Philadelphia District Attorney Lynn Abraham. The newspaper noted that Segal "comes on like a hyperactive teddy bear." The *Philadelphia Inquirer*'s *Today* magazine commented in 1974 that Segal made sure that public officials, TV personalities, and the Philadelphia police realized that that he was a force to be reckoned with. "Besides racing through TV studios disrupting Johnny Carson's *Tonight Show* and Walter Cronkite's *CBS Evening News,* Segal has chained himself up at various buildings around Philadelphia, including Independence Hall, in order to dramatize his protest against the shoddy treatment of homosexuals by the heterosexual ruling class." (Courtesy William Way Archives and Library.)

Participants during the dedication liturgy of the Metropolitan Community Church's new building on Fairmount Avenue on October 4, 1981, include, from left to right, Leslie Phillips, Rev. Frank Crouch and his partner Rev. Bruce Hughes, and Marianne Van Fossen (seated). Van Fossen has since become an ordained minister. (Courtesy Gail Didich.)

Au Courant photographer Terri Suomi captured an upsetting message on a Center City street. The sentiment, among some, remains unchanged since the Annual Reminder and Stonewall. In 1975, for instance, the *Weekly Gayzette* reported that former Philadelphia resident Bernie Boyle had filed suit against the city seeking $100,000 damages for injuries received during a lecture given by Dr. David Reuben at the Playhouse in the Park. "Boyle was requested to leave the Playhouse by several Police officers after he attempted to question Dr. Reuben, who is author of a best-seller containing material which many gay people consider inaccurate and derogatory," the Gazette said. "While complying with the police, Boyle was hit on the head with a nightstick and was knocked unconscious. The attack caused a head wound requiring ten stitches." (Courtesy William Way Archives and Library.)

Darrel David, shown with a popular Egyptian decoration, was Tyrone Smith's companion for many years. (Courtesy Tyrone Smith.)

At a party in the 1970s, a jubilant Mark Segal joins in a toast with Sally Tyre, then an advertising representative for *Philadelphia Gay News* and manager for Mamzelle's Bar, on 12th Street. (Courtesy Mel Heifetz.)

For years, Mary the Hat was a fixture in various gay bars. Tall and regal, she had a grandmotherly appeal. Gay men loved her and doted on her. The heterosexual matron never missed happy hour in one or several gay bars. One saw her in the blistering heat making her way to Woody's, or bracing herself against high winds, her hands gripped on the walker as the wind blew her frail body backwards like an animated figure. Nothing stopped Mary the Hat from her Don Quixote quest for cocktails and the company of gay men until her untimely death in the 1990s. (Courtesy William Way Archives and Library.)

Frank Broderick, a 1976 graduate of Pennsylvania State University, was a dedicated journalist for six years and a columnist for the *Philadelphia Gay News* (*PGN*) before publishing *Au Courant* as an alternative to *PGN*, the city's only gay and lesbian newspaper. Broderick's widely read *PGN* column "Trash" assured *Au Courant* an instant readership. Broderick was publisher and editor; his staff included Jeffrey Wilson, Mike Labance, Larry Bush, Brandon Judell, David MacDonald, and Steve Warren. "The name says it all," Broderick stated in the premier issue. "Au Courant means informed on current affairs; up to the minute. And that's what we'll be doing for our readers . . . we'll be doing a better job of it than others can." For years, *Au Courant* and *PGN* were competitive rivals, never missing opportunities to slight one another in print in the game of one-upmanship. Yet most gay and lesbian Philadelphians read both papers and seemed to appreciate each for its unique style and take on gay and lesbian life. Broderick, a lifelong train enthusiast, died from AIDS-related causes in the 1990s. *Au Courant* folded in 2000 after a noble last attempt to give Philadelphia an alternative news voice. (Courtesy Mel Heifetz.)

au courant

Promotional Sample

PHILLY GOES SILLY OVER NEW WEEKLY'S DEBUT

"While finding a single copy of 'Au Courant' may have resulted in strained vocal cords or a few fat lips, the hassle was worth it," the 1982 premier issue of *Au Courant* reported. (Courtesy Robert Schoenberg.)

Patrons enjoyed the free-spirited atmosphere of the Astral Plane Restaurant, where one could dine among crimson walls covered with photographs and autographs of silent film stars, Follies Bergere and Ziegfeld Follies greats. Past guests have included John F. Kennedy Jr., Bette Midler, Liza Minelli, Tommy Tune, Henry Fonda, and Mick Jagger. (Courtesy Reed R. Apaghian.)

A joyous looking Key West bar staff waves in unison near the Philadelphia Museum of Art. Key West opened in 1982 but, in 1989, owner Mel Heifetz closed the bar for a year and a half and eventually sold it. (Courtesy Mel Heifetz.)

The intense synergy between performance artists Greg Giovanni (left) and Tomas Dura makes itself felt in this scene from *The Balloon and The Angel*. Dura, who studied flamenco dance with Jose Greco and taught clowning workshops in Belgium, is an international performer whose work has been staged in the Netherlands, Germany, London, and Toronto. He has also performed as a fire-eater, accompanied by a live orchestra. (Courtesy Tomas Dura; photography by Eric Toy.)

The Manayunk canal provides the backdrop for Giovanni and Dura in another still from *The Balloon and The Angel*. (Courtesy Tomas Dura; photography by Eric Toy.)

When the AIDS quilt came to Philadelphia in the 1980s, Philadelphians of every race and sexual orientation were moved to silence in the armory on 20th Street. One of the earliest AIDS cases in Philadelphia was of 29-year-old Steve McPartland. The April 15–21, 1983 edition of *Gay News* featured and quoted McPartland at length. (Courtesy William Way Archives and Library.)

When Pres. George Bush came to Philadelphia in 1991, ACT UP, including Scott Tucker (second from the right) participated in a huge demonstration on Broad Street. A simple coffin was carried around and stirred up mixed emotions. The media reported that the coffin had nicked a police officer; the police say demonstrators threw bottles. A scuffle ensued, and several demonstrators were injured and arrested by police. (Courtesy William Way Archives and Library.)

In 1991, Act Up raided the offices of the *Welcomat*. The raid was a protest over "Your bodies, yourselves," a controversial front-page essay by Patrick Hazard. Act Up had demanded a rebuttal also be published on page one. *Welcomat* editor Dan Rottenberg (left) replied that he would consider Act Up's article but made no promise about its placement or even to publish it at all. Fallout occurred when the paper's gay restaurant reviewer resigned in protest. The paper was condemned in the gay press and, in time, Act Up mounted a boycott to persuade gay *Welcomat* advertisers to switch their ads elsewhere. Scott Tucker (right) a gay health activist and journalist, was part of the Act Up contingent that confronted Rottenberg about Hazard's essay. Tucker is the author of *The Queer Question: Essays on Desire and Democracy.* (Courtesy William Way Archives and Library.)

Dr. John L. Turner (upper right) delivers a lecture on HIV-AIDS to a group of health care professionals and AIDS activists. An endocrinologist with offices on Walnut Street, Turner was among a handful of physicians in the city in the 1980s who treated AIDS patients with a non-judgmental attitude. The openly gay physician was born in Boise, Idaho, on a farm. "I don't mind you saying it was a dreary childhood, yes, it was dreary. In school I was popular and politically successful as you can be without being a jock, and once out of the University of Washington in Seattle I married my high school sweetheart," Turner said to a reporter. About AIDS, Turner is quoted as having said, "We're not going to be killed because we're not going to let ourselves die." (Courtesy William Way Archives and Library.)

Gail Didich came to Philadelphia from western Pennsylvania in the mid-1970s. She joined Sisterspace, a lesbian feminist organization, in the late 1970s. "The first serious debate we had at Sisterspace was about transgendered people who . . . considered themselves women," Didich recalls. She joined Philadelphia Metropolitan Community Church in 1981 and was ordained a deacon by the Reverend Troy Perry, who had founded the church in October 1971. Didich is shown at a Franklin Institute party on World AIDS Day. (Courtesy Gail Didich.)

Larry Gross, Ph.D. (center), author and Philadelphia Lesbian and Gay Task Force (PLGTF) cochair, and Rita Addessa (right), task force executive director, are shown at another one of the task force's myriad news conferences. PLGTF began in 1978 to advance civil, human, and constitutional rights for gay and lesbian people; bisexual and transgendered people were later added. In 1982, PLGTF spearheaded a city-wide movement to amend the Philadelphia Fair Practices Act, known as Bill 1358, to include lesbian, gay, bisexual, and transgender people despite opposition from the Catholic archdiocese. In 1986, the task force released the first citywide "Study of Discrimination and Violence Against Lesbian and Gay People." PLGTF also staffs a Discrimination and Violence Hotline project. Gross is the author of *Up From Invisibility: Lesbian, Gay Men, and the Media in America.* (Courtesy PLGTF.)

Recording artist Anthony Louis (left) met Robert Cary Baysa at Philadelphia's Gay Coffeehouse in the early 1980s. Their Holy Union ceremony was performed by the Rev. Joseph Gilbert of Philadelphia's Metropolitan Community Church. Louis says that he willingly gave up his music career to devote quality time to his marriage. (Courtesy Anthony Louis.)

Rev. Joseph Gilbert (left), pastor of Philadelphia's Metropolitan Community Church in the 1980s, is shown with his partner, Michael. (Courtesy Gail Didich.)

The multitalented William J. Way speaks to a gathering at the first Philadelphia AIDS Walk in 1987. The American University graduate was hired by the city in 1965 as an urban-renewal technician. He later administered renewal work in the model cities area of North Philadelphia and, during the Rizzo administration, served as project manager for the Washington Square West Renewal Project. Way's most notable accomplishment was his work relocating businesses from the Center City convention center area. Way was influential in getting then Mayor Goode to declare June 26 as AIDS Awareness Day. He fought attempts to keep his illness from AIDS a secret and generally helped to educate the public in resisting attempts to cover up AIDS-related deaths. (Courtesy Marge McCann.)

A.J. turned heads whenever he strolled city streets, including those of Philadelphia's tenderloin district, which included scores of small bars, strip joints, and peep shows. Filbert Street in the 1960s and 1970s was a neon candy land at night. During the day, businessmen, city hall employees, and blue-collar workers would flood these fly-by-night quarter palaces. At night, bars like the Track Seven provided refuge for Greyhound bus travelers, ordinary citizens, sailors, old queens, bums, hustlers, and Janis Joplin jukebox fans. All night long these denizens would prowl from the Filbert Street strip down 13th Street to Arch Street, where groups would congregate on corners and camp it up till the wee hours. In the pre-AIDS era, sex was seen by some as a form of fast food. (Courtesy Tyrone Smith.)

In 1989, Paul Woodyard began a list of friends who had died from HIV or AIDS. As Woodyard was a member of the Philadelphia Gay Men's Chorus, many of the names on the list included his fellow chorus members. After Woodyard died in 1995, his partner Joel Kaylor continued the list. Woodyard does not appear in this photograph of the chorus taken in the 1980s.

Harvard-educated and divorced father of two Walter J. Lear (left) worked for the state health department in the 1980s and 1990s. Lear was the first public official in the city and the state of Pennsylvania to announce his homosexuality. In 1993, Lear stood up and turned his back to Gen. Colin Powell (to protest the defense department's banning gays from the military) when Powell spoke to the 50th reunion of the Harvard Class of 1943. Lear was later the 1998 recipient of the Bread and Roses Community Fund's Paul Robeson Social Justice Award. (Courtesy PLGTF; photography by A. Villanova.)

The founding members of Unity Philadelphia are, from left to right, Gregory Williams, Brett M., and Arnold Jackson. Founded in 1986 to deal with issues of HIV/AIDS in the African American Community, Unity flourished in the city during Mayor Wilson Goode's administration. The end of Mayor Frank Rizzo's reign brought smiles to the faces of political progressives, most African Americans, and the majority of gays and lesbians. (Courtesy Tyrone Smith.)

In June 1983, Stanley Ward (left), a native of Roanoke, Virginia, was named editor of the *Philadelphia Gay News*. Ward, who earned a Ph. D. from Harvard, was no uptight academic when it came to iconoclastic journalism. In 1984, he reminded readers of "the destructive role played by the Catholic Church, in New York and Philadelphia as well as elsewhere, in the effort to secure legislative protection for the rights of gays and lesbians." Ward condemned Philadelphia's mayor, the Human Relations Commission, and the city's legal department for their refusal to challenge the bigotry of the archdiocese. With Ward is writer Victoria Brownworth. (Courtesy PLGTF.)

The Key West baseball team was photographed in a robust, virulent pose *c.* the 1980s.

Philadelphia's vibrant leather community rose to the fore in the 1980s. Mark Danley, Philadelphia's 1983 Mr. Leather (center) is flanked by expertly outfitted friends and fellow contestants. Frank McGowan (front left) was for several years the "Leathering Up" columnist for *Philadelphia Gay News*. Ron Lord (lower right), one-time owner and manager of the city's only leather bar, the Bike Stop, celebrated the opening of the bar by hanging a motorcycle from the ceiling. (Courtesy William Way Archives and Library.)

Joe Moore, a bartender at the Smart Place, an African American bar on Sansom Street, greets customers on Halloween. Because of their isolation from mainstream gay white culture, African American gay bars were located near the strip. The Ritz was the most famous. Located midway between Arch and Market Streets, the corner bar attracted rich and poor, white and black, the out and closeted. The Ritz began as a straight bar, but gay men started coming in droves until all the straight men stopped coming. Pentoney's was another African American bar on Arch Street that attracted gay men, lesbians, pimps, and voyeurs who wanted to view the cavalcade. (Courtesy Tyrone Smith.)

Then candidate for mayor W. Wilson Goode (third from the left) was photographed at a May 9, 1983 gala sponsored by Lesbian and Gay Friends of Wilson Goode and Equus. Equus, a gay bar at 12th and Spruce Streets (now the 12th Street Air Command), was the consummate gay male watering hole in the 1980s. Tony Silvestre (left), chair of the Governor's Council on Sexual Minorities and director of the Eromin Center, stands beside at-large city council candidate John Anderson, a prominent member of Philadelphia City Council in the late 1970s. David Fair (right) was the founder of Lesbian and Gay Friends. The event raised $20,000 for the Goode campaign. Goode was a friend to the gay community and eventually won the race. (Courtesy William Way Archives and Library.)

The owners of Philadelphia's Waldorf Café, Paul Arcure (left) and Eric Dietrich, strike an intimate pose at work. The Waldorf Café, at 2000 Lombard Street, was the first host city restaurant for Dining Out for Life, an AIDS benefit in which participating restaurants donate 33 percent of gross food sales to AIDS charities. (Courtesy William Way Archives and Library.)

In 1984, an organization called Lesbian and Gays Against Censorship distributed flyers throughout Center City. Among many other facts, the flyer reported that "Giovanni's Room received numerous death threats and hundreds of obscene phone calls after patrons submitted an objectionable pamphlet carried by the store to a city council member. The council member demanded an investigation into possible criminal activity, and the investigation was reported in local media. The ensuing panic resulted in bomb threats and eventually broken windows. (Courtesy William Way Archives and Library.)

Actor Martin Sheen (center) and Tyrone Smith (left) visit with a resident of the Burning Bush, an AIDS hospice on Baltimore Avenue in West Philadelphia c. 1980. The Burning Bush, which had a high number of African American residents, remained open until the late 1980s, supported by UNITY and a number of other HIV/AIDS groups." (Courtesy Tyrone Smith.)

From 1969 until 1971 the Homophile Action League, Gay Liberation Front, and Radical Lesbians were the city's most important gay and lesbian groups. Local leftist weeklies such as the *Plane Dealer* (later called the *Gay Dealer*) and the *Drummer* provided broad coverage to the challenge that lesbians and gay men directed toward city government, especially the police. Shown at the March on Washington for Lesbian and Gay Rights on October 11, 1987, are, from left to right, unidentified, Rita Addessa, three unidentified persons, and Ado Bello.

Rita Addessa (left) discusses the difficulty in obtaining demonstration permits during the 1986 Constitution Celebration near Independence Hall. "When 200 Congress people were coming to Philadelphia, there was paranoia among the local police, the state police, the federal police, and the White House police [due to a visit from Pres. Ronald Reagan] . . . When the protest was finally allowed, there were more police and sharpshooters than there were protesters." (Courtesy PLGTF.)

The Lesbian and Gay Bill of Rights is a huge scroll created by Philadelphia Lesbian and Gay Task Force for the impromptu We the People U.S. Constitution demonstration at Independence Hall. In 1986, the U.S. Supreme Court decreed that in the Bowers v. Hardwick case, a Georgia gay man was not entitled to protection against prosecution for violating that state's anti sodomy laws. The court's decision, which essentially allowed the law to break into the privacy of an individual's bedroom, caused a storm of protest throughout the nation. (Courtesy PLGTF.)

Reed R. Apaghian (center) and his Astral Plane drag bride electrify another costume party at the restaurant c. 1980s. (Courtesy Reed R. Apahgian.)

Dan Martin (right) and his partner, Michael Biello, have been together for 26 years. Martin came to Philadelphia in 1974 and worked in Giovanni's Room; he also did illustrations for the *Weekly Gayzette*. The Martin and Biello creative team created the male musical *X-posed* in 1984, the year this photograph was taken. With Biello as codirector, Martin composed the music, wrote most of the lyrics, and acted in the show. "[Martin's] ballads are quite moving torch songs, and he has a gift for patter songs that are catchy and yet have something to say," wrote the *Philadelphia Inquirer* during the musical's run at the Walnut Street Theater. (Courtesy Dan Martin.)

Flushing in unison are, from left to right, Patrick McGinley, Bill Riches, and Paul Woodyard, taking time out from their portrayal of the Linoleum Sisters at Henri David's 1987 Halloween Ball at the Warwick Hotel. McGinley, according to friend Joel Kaylor, "was the instigator of many hilarious escapades, parties, and events, such as the infamous Palm Sunday parties." (Courtesy Joel Kaylor.)

One of the first gay African American street fairs was held on Sansom Street in 1986. Organized by the clientele of Stars, an African American bar, and UNITY president Tyrone Smith, the fair gave African Americans an opportunity to separate from the larger gay community. A motivating force behind the fair was club owner Joey Venuti, who worked with Henri David in the early 1970s on Miss Philadelphia contests. (Courtesy Tyrone Smith.)

120

Philadelphia's legendary W. Thacher Longstreth, a city councilman-at-large and two-time Republican candidate for mayor, speaks with gay activists in city hall c. the 1980s. Longstreth's grandmother, the indomitable Ella Hoover (Gah) Thacher, was a leading temperance crusader in the 1930s. Once a vocal opponent of most gay rights issues in city council, Longstreth did an about-face and now considers himself a friend of the lesbian, gay, bisexual, and transgender community. (Courtesy William Way Archives and Library.)

Joel Kaylor, a Philadelphia artist and for years one of the chief organizers of the Gay and Lesbian Arts Festival (GALA), is related to the poet Walt Whitman. According to Kaylor, however, nobody in his family ever wanted to talk about Whitman. "It's almost as if the feeling was 'if we don't talk about him he won't exist in our family.' They probably knew he was queer. I'm sure they did, that's why it's been like pulling teeth to get my father, who's in his 90s, to talk about Whitman. According to Kaylor, Whitman organized an "erotic circle of male nurses, soldiers and patients who found time and places to play with each other" when the poet regularly visited wounded or dying Civil War soldiers in Ward K of Washington's Armory Square Hospital in 1863. (Courtesy Joel Kaylor.)

This is a rousing scene at the 1984 City of Brotherly Love Softball League (CBLSL) championship league playoffs, in which the Bike Stop beat Woody's. (Courtesy John Edgar.)

The second Burger protest after the Supreme Court decision in Bowers v. Hardwick, the landmark Georgia sodomy case, was named the Burger Roast (for Supreme Court Justice Warren Burger) by African American poet and activist Julie Blackwoman. (Courtesy PLGTF.)

Woody's women's softball champions of the City of Brotherly Love Softball League Women's Division 1995 assemble on a Center City step. Betty Long (front row, fourth from the left) and her sister Christine wrote a sports column for the *Philadelphia Gay News* for a year before they were picked up by *Au Courant*. Betty Long was the first woman commissioner of CBLSL from 1997 to 1998. (Courtesy Betty Long.)

Poet Allen Ginsberg puts his "queer shoulder to the wheel" while walking on Philadelphia's Market Street with former Channel 29 news director Roger Le Mey. Ginsberg was in Philadelphia to read at the Walt Whitman Cultural Arts Center in Camden. (From "America," by Allen Ginsberg; Courtesy Lamont Steptoe.)

In a Center Square elevator are, from left to right, poet Aaren Yeatts Perry, writer James Baldwin, and poet Lamont Steptoe after a meal at the skyscraper restaurant. (Courtesy Lamont Steptoe.)

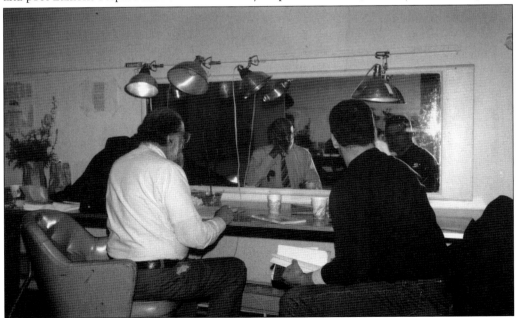

Allen Ginsberg checks out his reflection in the green room of the Painted Bride Art Center and sees Narcissus in the form of poet Jim Cory, who in turn stares into the eye of the camera. "I saw you, Walt Whitman, childless, lonely old grubber, poking among the meats in the refrigerator and eyeing the grocery boys," Ginsberg wrote. "I heard you asking questions of each: Who killed the pork chops? What price bananas? Are you my Angel?" (Courtesy Lamont Steptoe.)

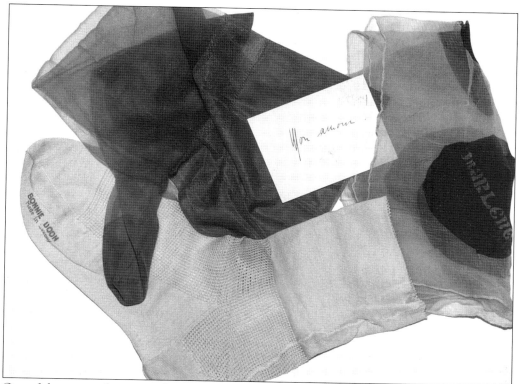

One of the personal items in the Rosenbach Museum and Library's Gay and Lesbian Literature and History Collection is a pair of silk stockings and a handkerchief given to Mercedes de Acosta by Marlene Dietrich. With a note signed "Mon Amour," Dietrich was clearly under de Acosta's spell.

In 1999, I interviewed Montreal resident John Banks, who for 12 years was Dietrich's personal assistant both in the United States and Europe. A self-described Dietrich freak since he was 12, Banks met the film legend at age 15 while standing in line for an autograph. Impressed by the boy's observations about her recordings, Dietrich invited him to accompany her entourage back to Montreal's Ritz-Carlton.

"Dietrich had a soft spot for Mercedes de Acosta, and once sent her one of her own silk stockings. De Acosta was very much into her affair with Garbo at the time and was not responsive," Banks says.

"De Acosta wrote in her memoirs [*Here Lies the Heart* (1960)] about her affair with Garbo and her friendship with Dietrich. She wrote about how Marlene was bewitched by her in a way. Maria, Marlene's daughter, wrote in her book that Marlene had an affair with Mercedes. But I met Mercedes. Unfortunately, she was a little old lady with crutches at the time—she was a little withered thing—but Marlene was terribly fond of her still. She covered her with kisses. We talked a lot about Mercedes because her book had just come out—this was 1965, I guess—and Marlene liked de Acosta's book. She said: 'Finally, there's a book about a woman who was born in the upper crust and rich and wrote about her rich life rather than somebody who comes from down and goes up.'" (Courtesy William Way Archives and Library.)

Alexandra Grilikhes has taught creative writing, memoir writing, and women studies at the University of the Arts in Philadelphia for more than two decades. For ten years, she hosted the only literary programs in Philadelphia, on public radio. As director of the University of Pennsylvania's Annenberg School of Communications Library, she organized and produced five groundbreaking international festivals of films by women at the university. Her stories, essays, and poetry appear in the *Seattle Review*, *Fish Drum*, and "The Lesbian Review of Books." She is also editor/publisher of the national literary/arts journal, *American Writing; A Magazine*. She was nominated for the Pushcart Prize in fiction. Her novel *Yin Fire* was published in 2001.

Charley Engel (left) a concert pianist, and Albert Lister met on the campus of the University of Pennsylvania in 1948. The couple say they were friends for one and a half years before they "acted out something" but continued to date girls because they were not sure they were gay. They struggled for several years with monogamy issues but say that AIDS put an end to that. In 1983, the *Philadelphia Inquirer* told their story, using pseudonyms, as a gay couple who had been together for 35 years. (Courtesy Charley Engel and Albert Lister.)

Debra D'Alessandro, left, host of Philadelphia's WYBE-TV's lesbian and gay show *Philly Live!*, is in bed with Butch Cadora, gay talk show host of DUTV's (Drexel University) *In Bed with Butch*. D'Alessandro, who also hosts the lesbian Amazon Country show on WXPN-FM radio, has a relaxed style and often breaks into mainstream themes to attract larger, heterosexual audiences. Cadora came up with the idea of hosting a talk show from bed while talking to friends at a party. His guests have included the famous and the infamous. Says Cadora: "I want to be as famous as Oprah!" Philadelphia's *Under the Pink Carpet*, with host Tony Swicki, is also aired on WYBE-TV.

Robert Schoenberg, University of Pennsylvania teacher, activist, and founder of ActionAids in 1986, is the author of *With Compassion Toward Some: Homosexuality and Social Work in America*, published in 1984 by Harrington Park Press.

Donald Carter, Philadelphia's happy and progressive Log Cabin Republican, was once a guest on Bill Mahr's *Politically Incorrect*. He is shown in 1999 at the Astral Plane. The woman in the photograph is not identified.

The largest gay and lesbian national writers conference, Behind Our Masks III, was held in Philadelphia in 2000. Three of the attendees are, from left to right, Felice Picano, Thom Nickels, and Andrew Holleran.